What they're s and t

MW01269092

"The West Orange Chamber of Commerce is proud to be connected with Mike O'Keefe, Scott Girard and Marc Price of **Expert Business Advice**. Their dynamic presentations, intellectual wealth, and unique insight into small business have helped numerous Chamber members take their businesses to the next level."

Krista Compton Carter, IOM

West Orange Chamber of Commerce Vice President

Winter Garden, Florida, USA

"I've had the pleasure of working with Michael O'Keefe on many projects over the years. His ability to evaluate situations, identify competitive advantage opportunities and implement well thought-out strategic plans is second to none."

Jim Costello

Director of Project Management

Marriott International Design & Construction Management

"Marc Price is a business builder! I have seen him start with a blank piece of paper and create a million dollar business for a financial education online application and service. He is a natural network builder and relationship marketer who works hard, is very creative, and who usually surpasses all objectives for sales, service, and market share growth. You want Marc on your team if your goal is to grow your brand and increase top and bottom lines."

Mike Schiano, MA, CRHC, CPFC

Information and Technology Services

BUSINESS FINANCE BASICS

CRASH COURSE for ENTREPRENEURS

BUSINESS FINANCE BASICS

Learn What You Need in Two Hours

Scott L. Girard, Jr., Michael F. O'Keefe
and Marc A. Price

Series Editor: Scott L. Girard, Jr.

A Crash Course for Entrepreneurs—From Expert Business Advice

Starting a Business

Sales and Marketing

Managing Your Business

Business Finance Basics

Business Law Basics

Franchising

Value-Driven Business

Time and Efficiency

International Business

Supplemental Income

Social Media

Web-Based Business

Copyright © 2014, Scott L. Girard, Jr., Michael F. O'Keefe, and Marc A. Price

ISBN: 978-90-77256-40-4

The Expert Business Advice trademark is owned by Expert Business Advice, LLC and is used under license. www.expertbusinessadvice.com

Distributed by Career Press, Inc., 220 West Parkway, Unit 12, Pompton Plains, NJ 07444, U.S.A., www.careerpress.com

D/2014/9797/1

Printed in the United States of America

20 19 18 17 16 15 14 13 12 11 10 9 8 7 6 5 4 3 2

Cover design: Bradford Foltz

Text design: Softwin

For Kathe

Contents

Foreword

You can spot entrepreneurs easily when they talk about their businesses and dreams. Their passion and fascination with their business—and others' businesses—is remarkable. When I met Scott, Mike and Marc, I knew before they told me about the 17 businesses they've collectively started that these were talented, insightful, seasoned entrepreneurs. We quickly agreed to develop the Crash Course for Entrepreneurs together.

The aim of this series is to give you high-level overviews of the critical things you need to know and do if you want to start (or you're already running) your own business. In a two-hour read. Of course, there's much more to know about every topic covered, but we believe that what you'll read here will give you the framework for learning the rest. A Resources section and a Glossary will ensure you can ground yourself in the essentials. And www.expertbusinessadvice.com, the co-authors' website, offers expanded support for entrepreneurs that is updated daily.

Entrepreneurs vary widely in what they want to do. Your dream may be to start a very small, one-person service, perhaps doing home maintenance or day care or accounting from your home. You may have developed or discovered a high-tech breakthrough that will need years of testing and dozens or hundreds of people to bring to market. This book sees the intrinsic value and challenges of both styles of business. It will definitely help you make the most of your opportunity, whatever its scale.

Most of the chapters in this book represent the authors' collective experience and point of view, but a few are personal pieces. You'll find the initials of each author at the end of those. Here's a brief word from each of them.

I remember when I fully understood what our series of books should accomplish. Mike, Marc and I had recently decided that we wanted to write a series of books for people only moderately familiar with entrepreneurship and business. Multitudes of books already exist on basic levels of business practices and procedures. We knew that writing another one of those books wouldn't really serve anyone or change anything, no matter how well written it was.

On the morning that I "got it," I was drinking coffee and reading the news; the television was on in the background. I glanced up and saw a commercial for a foreign language software program in which, instead of learning by simply repeating vocabulary, the student is culturally immersed in the language, holistically surrounded with concepts of all manner of things applicable to the subject. In short, they don't list facts and terms and call it teaching—they show the student a vast array of information, on a multitude of levels, allowing her to bathe in knowledge.

I knew then that instead of presenting a bunch of facts that we think you should know about business, we should take a more holistic approach and help you immerse yourself in business thinking. Our method is most effective if you read this book cover to cover, skipping nothing. If you reach a section and either think it doesn't address your needs, or you think you know everything there is to know about the subject, read it anyway. It'll only take a minute—that's why the sections are not lengthy. It will enlighten and organize your thinking, either way. You'll see important concepts woven through various discussions, as they holistically fit in.

If you're hoping to read a book and immediately become the world's greatest business person, this book isn't for you. If your goal, however, is to quickly understand and feel familiar with the basics of starting a business, as your first stepping-stone to greatness, we believe that our book has no rival.

I sincerely hope that this book will not only increase your understanding of entrepreneurship and basic business finance, but that it also gives you pleasure and satisfaction as you learn the key principles and language of business.

Scott L. Girard, Jr.

When we sat down and decided to take on the daunting task of writing a series of books for entrepreneurs and small business owners, I cringed. I thought, "How can we ever reduce our advice and experiences to writing? And how can we cover it all—can we fit it into a book?"

Either way, we decided to get started, so each of us began drafting sections related to our respective specialties and work experience. Only as the initiative continued did I discover a certain passion for sharing my advice in a personal way, trying to convey how it felt to go places, negotiate situations, and experience new things, both good and bad, in the course of starting businesses.

I take the same approach with business as I did with competitive sailing with my father when I was a kid. It's all about constant adjustment. You don't just rig the boat and go. It's about looking around, reading the wind, and predicting shifts and changes before they happen—just like understanding the external forces that affect a business or industry. While doing so, you are constantly looking around at other boats, just like you'd do benchmarking against other competitors in business—analyzing their speed and angle and comparing it to your own. Most often, what gets a boat (or business) ahead isn't some significant advantage; it's the inches or degrees of adjustment and the teamwork that generates the results. If you can point just a little higher or generate just a little more boat speed, it can make all the difference in the world—just like in business. If the organization can run just a little bit more efficiently, demonstrate better teamwork, identify the out-in-front opportunities, and not "just kind of want it" but rather, do anything to win, it will be the most likely to succeed.

I hope that this book will capture your interest, provide valuable information, and share an interesting perspective into the world of starting businesses and managing their finances.

Mike F. O'Keefe

Everyone has heard the phrase "Knowledge is Power." I would have it read "Information is Power," for a couple of reasons.

We live in an age of instant information about every facet of our lives. We can receive news, on-demand weather and traffic reports, sports scores, social media happenings, and stock market updates. And yet, we forget much of this information within moments of receiving it, as new reports and updates are constantly replacing the data we were just beginning to process.

Most generic information travels fast these days. On the other hand, some information is meant to stay with us for a while, if not forever. And with that in mind, Scott, Mike and I set out to write a series of books to deliver lasting, valid information for entrepreneurs and small business owners.

Our passion for success in business and in life lies behind every page we write. As life-long, serial entrepreneurs, we have always taken the approach of surrounding ourselves with information, ideas and viewpoints from countless sources to support our efforts in constructing our next project. That information, when reliable and trustworthy, can and will be used over and over for repeated success. So, in essence, information is power, when applied over time.

Our series of books represents the hard work, research and application of numerous business philosophies, ideas and viewpoints. You will find rock-solid information that can be applied now…and later. It's information that can be shared, and then referred to as a refresher down the road, if needed. Our goal was to deliver information and advice that is *relevant, smart and timely. We hope these fresh, contemporary approaches to the fundamentals of business finance will get you, and keep you, at the top of your game.*

The way forward begins here…

Marc A. Price

We all hope this book supports the fire and drive you feel now as you think about starting or confront the realities of running your own business and its finances day to day. And we wish you success.

Kathe Grooms
Managing Director, Nova Vista Publishing

CHAPTER I
Getting Off to a Strong Start

Staging Your Business for Financial Success

*It's not black magic, though sometimes a
little magic might help!*

IT'S SAFE TO SAY that the great majority of entrepreneurs who start their first business are pretty ignorant about finance. That's nothing to be ashamed of; we live in times when our education and preparation for the work world are pretty tightly focused. You're no doubt pretty passionate and proficient in the area on which your business operates. And that matters, a lot.

So if you didn't have a finance and accounting background, it's going to be one of your challenges to get educated about the aspects of finance that affect your business (and your industry sector). But the good news is that, for many entrepreneurs, even non-number people, their *own* numbers become really fascinating. Your business's finances are part of the score card by which you and others measure your success.

There's another piece of good news here too. There is a wealth of targeted information out there to help you grasp and manage your business's finances. As you will soon read, there are professional accountants, bookkeepers, business support groups, government agencies, web sites, social media tribes, associations, clubs and more that you can tap for expertise and advice, not to mention money. Your banker, customers, colleagues, competitors and of course family and friends may be unexpected sources of wisdom. We don't pretend this book will give you all you need to succeed, but we do believe it will map the world of business finance for you so you will know how to ask good questions and start figuring things out, including what you can do and what you'd best let specialists do for you.

In fact, we are here to help you in the next phase too, after you finish reading this book. If you'd like to drop us a line with a specific question (in English) related to the finance of your established or yet-to-be-launched business, we'll get back to you with a reply. Having started 17 businesses ourselves, to date, with more in our heads, we have quite a bit of pragmatic knowledge and plenty of experience, both good and bad, to make us confident we can either help directly or point you in the best possible direction. You'll find our email addresses in the About the Authors section at the end of this book.

We can imagine that you might find the info and advice herein a bit overwhelming if you are just starting out. But trust us, you *can* build a business step-by-step. And no matter how big or small that business may be, you can bet your successes will flow in part from the care you give to your business's financial health. So let's get started.

True Costs and Key Financial Drivers

Knowing the true costs of your products
or services is the only way to go.

ONE OF THE MOST IMPORTANT fundamentals to know about your business is the true cost of providing your products or services. It may seem like a basic point, but too many business owners have only a partial grasp of all the costs associated with delivering their products or services. The fully loaded cost to provide your product or service includes much more than just the direct cost of the materials and the labor to produce the offering.

When identifying the costs associated with preparing a product or service for sale, you need to include the proportional expense for every segment of the business that contributes to the creation of the product. This includes sales, marketing, facility overhead, management overhead, and all other expenses associated with operating the business. These are indirect expenses. They don't go up or down in association with an item's sale, compared to the direct costs that do.

It's worth pausing here for a reality check. It's possible you have been building your dream company with cocktail napkin calculations that look really good. If they don't include the items you have to pay for whether or not you sell a single thing, you could go broke sooner or later. It can be scary to confront fully loaded costs, but it's a lot more than scary to go bankrupt, so build your budgets and business plan taking their impact into account.

Allocating indirect costs

The challenge may be in identifying the appropriate portion of indirect expenses associated with a given product or service. The best approach may be to determine the current or potential portion of total sales that it represents in your entire offering. If your intent is to price all items with a similar profit margin, it would be appropriate to assign indirect expenses based on the percentage of total sales revenue an item contributes. So if the product or service you are pricing is expected to provide 20 percent of the sales volume, you would allocate 20 percent of the indirect expenses of your company.

Now compute the indirect expense associated with each individual item in your offering, based on your proportional allocations above. Add your direct material and labor costs to each allocated expense, and you'll have the fully loaded cost of each of your products or services. Once you have made this calculation of fully loaded cost, you will have a proper basis for understanding the profitability of each product or service you bring to market. It is only after you have a clear understanding of your fully loaded costs will you be able to identify the real profit potential of a product or service.

With a clear picture of all your fully loaded costs, you will be better able to monitor and adjust product development, target sales and marketing initiatives and stage your business to achieve consistent profitability. When a particular product or service falls short of your expectations, you will be able to adjust sales volume, product pricing, or product development with other products to fill the gap and maintain or exceed profit targets for your business. That way, an item that falls short of expected sales volume might be offset by increased sales volume of another better-performing one. Monitoring the performance of all items and knowing their actual impact to company profitability is essential for you to maintain the expected financial performance of your company.

This essential piece, your product performance information, is part of what helps you stage your business for financial success. The other pieces, which we call your key financial drivers, include those items that have the greatest impact to your emerging and long-term financial success. In each business this list may be different, but on it you will see the items that can make or break your best-laid plans. Don't get distracted by smaller, less relevant numbers if they steal time and effort away from evaluating these key ones. Key financial drivers may include:

- Payroll
- Travel and entertainment
- Advertising
- Marketing
- Consulting (including your legal and financial advice)
- Cost of goods, freight
- Rent and utilities
- Finance charges, bank fees, etc.

Monitoring these numbers on a daily, weekly and monthly basis is key to being able to identify problems and opportunities and make changes that will allow you to optimize your business's financial success at all times. Identifying fully loaded costs combined with a disciplined method of tracking and responding to your key financial drivers will stage your business for optimum financial success.

Building a Foolproof Budget

In the beginning, keep it simple! The real value
of a business budget is being able to see where
your money comes in and goes out.

BUSINESS BUDGETS are not always fun to build. Until a budget has saved you and your business from disaster, there's a good chance you won't fully appreciate one for what it is. For a very small business, a business budget might not seem necessary. You might think, "No worries, I just won't spend more than I make." Sounds like a good plan, at first. However, take it from me, as easy as it seems to manage a small business's finances without a budget, it is just as easy to find yourself looking at your business's bank account halfway through the year, asking yourself, "Where did all my money go?" You could even say that a small business needs a budget even more than a larger one, as it's so vulnerable to the slightest surprise.

Too often, a little more spent here plus a little more spent there can drop a ton of bricks out of the sky and kill a small business. Or it can cause you to have to pay out-of-pocket to get that last shipment in (or out), that last end-of-the-month bill cleared, or that last employee paid. Bottom line: running out of money before you plan to (which should be never) is the last thing you want to deal with.

Even if you're not faced with the dire situation of running completely out of money, to have less than you planned on is not good either. Remember it this way: Business is a competition. You are always competing with whoever controls other parts of whatever market you're in. A budget will help ensure you *can* get one more shipment out, run one more commercial or radio ad, cover payroll, get that company vehicle serviced, or even reward an exceptional employee with an unexpected bonus.

A business budget will help you streamline, stretch, and manage money effectively, and ensure you never run out unexpectedly. So even the smallest, newest business needs a budget, definitely before it starts up. Think about it: Do you really enjoy being clueless about how much money you have or where it's going?

What is a business budget?

Budgets are not black magic. A business budget is a tool that lets you track and maintain accountability of revenues (or receivables, the money you brought in), costs (payables, or money you spent), and profits (money you have left over after you paid all your bills, including salaries). A budget first of all shows you if your business is able to fund itself. If your trial budget comes out negative, that's a bummer, but it's a lot better than discovering that fact at the end of the year. It tells you you'll need to cut expenses or increase sales, or to tap other funding. So you can be pro-active without fearing that bad news will fall out of the sky.

Once you've set up a workable budget, you can monitor reality vs. your estimates. This allows you to watch your money on paper, and ensure you're not spending more than you're making. A budget can be managed by an accountant, but if you're just starting out, there's a good chance you can manage it yourself. There exist several great software tools that make the process even easier. (See pages 26 and 55).

Sales, costs and profit

The most basic budgets include sales and other revenues. This section will help you keep track of how much money you're making, and begin to build a history so you will be better able to predict sales trends in the future. Sales forecasts will come in handy if you're looking to expand your business, and will likely be required by your funder if you're going to try to take out a business loan or interest someone in investing in your company. The history you accumulate can also point to new opportunities, highlight cyclical highs and lows, and identify trends that can help or harm your success.

Of course, costs are also vital to track in order to ensure they don't get out of control and pull you into debt, or worse. In the same way your sales forecasts vs. actual sales reveals vital information, comparing your expense forecast with actual costs helps you refine your knowledge of your business's health. When you can see how much it actually costs to run your business, you can look more intelligently for ways to lower those costs to raise your overall profit!

That final part, profit, is everyone's favorite. Watching this part of your budget increase is like watching your bank account grow on payday, but it's *much* more rewarding. Profits are the fruits of your labor; you created this money! You can do whatever you please with this money: It's all yours! It might take you a while to actually get anything in this column of your budget, but when you do… Oh Boy! Mike, Marc and I still have the first dollar we ever made as business partners. It represents so much more than just a dollar. It represents something that we created together, and tells us that we are smarter and more capable as businessmen than *somebody*. Take my word for it, the first time you actually turn a profit as a business owner is like watching a child be born. But don't expect it to happen overnight.

To put things in perspective, most businesses don't turn a profit for up to three to five years. Don't let that scare you: The smaller and simpler your business, the quicker your profits will come. This is why, in our book *Starting a Business*, we suggest you start as small as possible and build from there. The risks and stress are lower, and you can actually have more fun with it.

In our business, we manage two budgets: monthly and annual. We review them monthly. The monthly budget is much more detailed and includes all of our expenses and every bit of income we receive. The annual budget, naturally more forward-looking and projective, helps us *see* on paper what we can and can't do with our money this year. For example, on our monthly budget, we ensure that we can pay our employees using the money we made this month. For the annual budget, we ensure that we don't hire more new employees than it suggests we will be able to afford at the end of the year. I use our employees as an example because they are the lifeblood of our business and our very top priority. Paid employees are happy employees and happy employees are what keep our business rockin' and rollin'. So it works out for everyone.

Why is a business budget important?

The great thing about a budget is that it keeps you honest and prevents many unpleasant surprises. It puts you in charge, and saves you from ignorantly responding to circumstances. You can *really see* what is happening in your business.

When I was a kid, I used to go to the county fair with my parents. My dad would give me some money to spend however I wanted. I could buy candy, ride rides, go to the petting zoo, play games, or do whatever else I wanted. After I spent that money, though, my willy-nilly fun was over, and I had to do whatever my parents wanted to do. So the first year, I spent all my money on the goldfish game, trying over and over and over to win that stupid goldfish (that no one *ever* wins). I wasn't able to play any other games, go into the petting zoo, ride any rides, or do any of the other fun things I wanted to do. Eventually, I after I cried for ten minutes, my mom slipped me a little more money and I was able to ride some rides. After that year I got smarter with my "budget" and had a lot more fun.

The same is true for you (and I hope that includes a good fairy who re-lines your pocket if you make the same mistake I made). When you're starting a business, you can't spend all your money on the greatest, most popular company cell phone or vehicle out there, because your business's money is extremely valuable, especially in the beginning. In business, when you're out of money, you're out of money and the game is over. A business budget is the best way to ensure you don't spend yourself into debt, and it helps you stretch your money to the max.

A final thought. Just because you build a monthly and annual budget doesn't mean you have to stick to it; it just means you can see it. While we don't often adjust our business's monthly budget (simply because a month in business goes by in the blink of an eye), we do often adjust our business's annual budget to accommodate new opportunities that present themselves throughout the year. Just because you create a budget doesn't mean you can't buy more cost-effective materials, hire employees at a lower salary if the market changes, or allocate more money to advertising if you get a great deal. Bottom line: Let your budget be your guide. Stay flexible, but within your business's means.

S.G.

Payment Term Basics

Don't let your customers treat you like an interest-free lender. Get paid, not played.

GETTING PAID can be tricky if you don't have the right payment terms in place, especially if you're new to business and your customer isn't. If you want to keep your business running smoothly, you should have vigorous payment controls to manage your cash flow and make money management a high priority. In order to avoid potentially lethal debts, from Day 1 put measures in place to help you keep track of, *and collect*, any money your business is owed.

Bank basics

First, you should open a bank account under your business's legal name. This is will give customers a means of paying you if they opt for direct deposit payment, and also keep your business's money away from your personal money. Opening an account will also make your work easy when it comes to making payments and filing taxes. And it will help you avoid transactions using liquid cash (paper money).

Ensure you open an account with a reputable bank that has nationwide or even international access, depending on your needs. Avoid new and up-and-coming banks that you don't recognize or banks that are run out of the back room of a tattoo parlor or a van down by the river. Activate your account by depositing some money into it. Also, as part of the account opening process, attach some credit to your account—just take care it's not more than you can reasonably afford to make payments on. A line of credit will come in handy when you need to make purchases or expand your business and you haven't yet collected everything in your accounts receivables (money customers owe you). Bear in mind that a typical overdraft protection line of credit may have a higher interest rate on the funds you use, compared to the rate on a straight loan, so try not to use that money for long periods of time.

Bookkeeping

You absolutely need to familiarize yourself with basic bookkeeping. That may sound scary, but it's essentially keeping track of where your money is: where it's coming from (or should be coming from), and where it's going. If you need schooling, look into evening classes, start-up support workshops, and read up on areas where you're weak. You need to have the most basic money management principles clear in your mind, even if you aren't doing the bookkeeping yourself. And you must understand credit, taxes, and bank statements to run your business intelligently.

Advanced bookkeeping is a challenge that many new entrepreneurs face. If you don't have master bookkeeping skills, retain or hire a professional accountant to help you maintain your business accounts. You can also invest in software that will help you track your business's cash flow. Software like QuickBooks will make the tracking of your finances easy and will allow you to create invoices, keep account information, handle payroll, and track your bank accounts. Some entrepreneurs install QuickBooks on their personal computers just to keep track of these key elements, in parallel but apart from what the accountant is doing, so they can come up with instant reports and snapshots of their business any time, day or night. Others set up access to the accountant's system so they can see actual data in real time.

As we've noted elsewhere in this book, if you use software like QuickBooks and you're not a trained accountant, get professional advice on how to set it up to accurately track your business.

References and quotes

Especially if your business is new, you may feel like anybody who orders from you is a welcome gift from above. But if your product or service is a high-ticket item or it requires a lot of investment before you deliver and invoice, it's entirely appropriate to ask a prospective customer for bank references. You probably have already filled out credit applications yourself, so consider them if you feel you need added protection against slow payers.

If your business is such that you prepare quotes for your customers, be sure to include the payment terms as part of them. If appropriate, also include such things as kill fees (when the customer stops a project before completion), late fees and partial payment schedules. Once you and your customer have agreed on all the details, ask the customer to sign and fax (or scan and email) you the quote sheet so you have a binding agreement. If you make a policy of not starting work on an order until you have the signed quote back, you won't risk a loss if the customer changes her mind and cancels the order. By requiring a signed quote (or purchase order) before you start work, you may gain a little leverage in the price negotiation, if the customer needs your product or service by a certain date.

Payment options and terms

For your company's survival and growth, you also need to be smart about the payment options you get from your own vendors and about terms you offer your own customers. Find out what the industry standard is, e.g., how everybody else in your industry is handling their payment terms. Obviously, the terms you negotiate with your vendors should be as favorable to you as possible.

On the income side, there are a number of payment modes you can allow your customers to use, such as cash, debit and credit cards, certified checks (we recommend staying away from personal checks), PayPal, and direct funds transfer. After you've done your homework on all this, sit down and come up with payment terms and debt collection regulations you will apply when you sell your product or service.

State and maintain strict rules regarding late payments from your customers, in line with your business sector. Put your terms on the back of every invoice and reference it on the front. Make sure to state clearly that the goods sold remain your property until the invoice is paid. Without this, in the case of a customer going bankrupt, you will have a hard time retrieving your goods from the customer's inventory and later on, you may only receive a fraction of their value—paid out over a period of years! Your invoices should also include the date payment is due, the amount, the modes of payment you offer, and your late payment fee schedule. With written terms, you will have something legally binding in case your customers don't pay on time or refuse to pay a late-payment fee.

Late payment fees

And don't be afraid to charge a late-payment fee; in fact, if you apply it absolutely rigorously, you'll save a lot of headaches. Also, don't let any of your customers give you a guilt trip about this fee. They knew the terms when they went into business with you. It's not personal; it's business. If you don't state any late-payment penalties, you may find that some customers will feel free to hold onto your money for a long period of time. You know what they're doing? Using you like a bank without paying you banking interest. And why wouldn't they? Again, it's not personal; it's just business! A late payment fee is like an interest rate that discourages customers from using your money too long, so go ahead state one—everybody else does.

Of course, there may be situations where you have a customer who's "too big to fail." They are either such big players that they call the shots, or they represent such a huge proportion of your business (something to avoid, generally) that they know they can disregard your late fee schedule. In these cases it's best to work closely with your accounts payable contact, or the top management, to try to put your case for prompt payment, or work out creative payment terms for an isolated situation. In the end, we feel it's best to have a late payment fee as a standard operating procedure. You can always vary or waive its terms as the situation dictates.

How do I stay on the offensive?

As we know, the timing of payments you receive for the products and services you offer will strongly influence the growth of your company as you build and grow it. If you don't get paid, you can't grow and, if that situation persists, you can go bankrupt. Even on a month-to-month basis, if you collect from your customers *before* you must pay your vendors, you can opt to use your line of credit for expansion or advertising, rather than for paying vendors. Or… maybe you can opt not to use credit at all, and save all that interest.

In addition to stipulating your late payment terms clearly on your invoices, you should also state the rules that apply in case of accumulated debts. With some customers you may have to establish a credit limit and not deliver goods or services they order when their open invoices exceed that limit.

Collections

When you have strict rules of payment, you naturally will prevent at least some late payments from occurring. Be quick to send late-paying customers a request for payment as soon as the payment is overdue. Automate this task via email if necessary (QuickBooks and similar programs can do this for you). This way, your customers will know that you are serious about collecting on time and will be less likely to fail to pay next time. The reward is critical: If you ensure that all your outstanding invoices are cleared, you have money to run your business. If you become lenient, customers can take advantage of you to pull your business down.

Sadly, there will always be those customers who tell you that they will pay in the future, but frankly, never do. The famous line from these customers is "the check is in the mail." Decide early how you are going to handle this and stick to your own terms.

Factoring and insuring invoices

Depending on the size of your business and the amount you invoice monthly, you might want to consider factoring to capture cash quickly. Factoring companies effectively buy your accounts receivable for approved customers (your customers whose records show them to be reliable payers) at a discount, paying you perhaps 70 percent to 80 percent of the invoice's value, less a service charge, in a matter of days. While you lose a big chunk to the factor, it may be better in cash crunch times than applying, waiting for approval, and finally receiving money from a bank in a straight loan. In factoring, the customer, not your company, is evaluated for credit worthiness. (They will want to know you've been in business for two years or more, and may have certain minimum monthly billing requirements, however.) If you think factoring might work for your short-term cash needs, educate yourself fully on it and get input from your accounting person before you sign up, and keep your use of factoring to a minimum.

There is also credit insurance. Again, for a fee, a credit insurance company will take over your invoice and pay an agreed portion of it to you, on time. They then attempt to collect from your customer themselves. Since their interest is to protect you, they try to research your customers and report any concerning information they discover to you. Some small businesses favor this service, as the reliability of cash flow can be important in your vulnerable early days. But do your math carefully before signing up, as the fees chew up your profits.

You can also insure your invoices specifically against the bankruptcy of your customers. As you know, if a customer declares bankruptcy, you may never receive payments due you, or get only 10 percent of the open invoice amounts in typical cases. To protect your company's exposure you can purchase insurance that covers around 75 percent to 80 percent of the invoice value, less a percent or two in service fees. In the event that customer goes belly up, the insurer will compensate you as agreed. You do not need to insure every customer, but it's worth considering if you are aware a given customer with a large open receivable (one who owes you a lot of money) is in financial trouble. Again, be careful, in your analysis, to see what the actual payment to you would be, vs. your profit margins. Low-margin businesses might erase all profit via the discounts off the invoice value mentioned above. But for many businesses, receiving a good share of an invoice's value vs. practically nothing in a bankruptcy is at least some help.

Once you have all your payment terms and policies, collections, and other financial protections in place, you can breathe (and rest) a little easier. And hopefully, watch the money that's due you come rolling in.

Preventing Cash Flow Worries and Woes

Being organized and disciplined are your humble miracle cures. Here are some tips to help keep your business in the black at all times.

AT ONE POINT or another, every business will run into cash flow problems. It's just the nature of business that you can't always predict the future, so accept that and move forward. New businesses are more vulnerable than established ones to both internal and external threats, but by far, the most common ones for them are cash flow problems. It pays off to run your business in ways that minimize the chances of negative cash flow so you only have to deal with the rest of the threats!

Cash flow basics

You'll find mountains of information and advice about cash flow in books, articles and blogs, so we will take the high-altitude view here to get you started. Just as with your household finances, you have income (receivables) and expenses (payables) in your business. While there are some technical uses of the phrase *cash flow*, for us it means the state of the balance between your income and expenses at any given moment. It's a snapshot, so it might describe today's balance, or next month's or next year's balance.

Positive cash flow means you have more cash and solidly reliable income—at that moment—than bills that need to be paid at that moment as well. *Negative cash flow* means you have more expenses to cover than the cash at your disposal.

To create your snapshot, whether of today's cash flow landscape or at some point in the future, you can use accounting software or even a cocktail napkin, calculator and pen. Let's say you need it for today, first of all. But you'll quickly see that this exercise will also start to map your future cash flow landscape as well.

Essentially the process goes like this:

- List all the cash assets your company has on hand today. Credit lines and promises to pay don't count; just list the cash you can use without going into debt.

- Now list all the payments you must make today: payroll, vendor invoices, taxes, rent, debt interest payments, and so forth. As you make this list you'll run into all the other bills you'll be facing in the coming months, so if you want to be efficient, chart them as well, in calendar fashion by date payable. This will start your future-focused cash flow report. The same is true for your receivables—you can chart them now too.

- Tally up today's bills and subtract that sum from your current cash total. If the result is positive, that number will go to the top of the next cash flow report, to which you'll add any payments received in the meantime, and that will become part of your cash assets for the next period. If your result is negative, it's time to get creative.

- Let's say you're negative but you have a credit line. You can dip into that, knowing (or hoping) some payments will come in to let you repay that loan quickly so you don't have a big interest bill to add to the rest of your obligations. Otherwise, you'll have to decide if any bills can be paid a little late (not recommended, but especially if you notify your debtor that you'll pay on X date and then do so, it might be okay) or if you need to raise more cash from all the other sources we've discussed in other sections.

- Take a look at your receivables due to come in in the future, and judge their certainty of being paid on time. Some payments are like gold: You know your government grant money will come in like clockwork, on the third day of every financial quarter. Others may be highly risky, either by being likely to come in late, or to be only partially paid, or to be heading toward bad debt (a huge reason to keep in touch with your customers!). Say that your current snapshot is negative, but that in the next two weeks you know that your grant money is due to come in, and it will cover today's shortfall. Taking a deep breath, you could conclude that you'll be okay for the next two weeks. Then you'll start the next report period with a zero balance, plus invoices you've made in the meantime. And this goes on and on into the future.

Cash Flow for Mary's Candy Shoppe				
	Jan.	Feb.	Mar.	Apr.
Starting Cash	1,000	1,200	900	(300)
Receivables				
Sales	1,000	1,100	1,200	1,300
Total Cash + Receivables	2,000	2,300	2,100	1,000
Payables				
Payroll	300	500	600	400
Overhead	300	400	400	400
Purchases	200	500	400	300
Capital Expenses	0	0	1,000	0
Total Payables	800	1,400	2,400	1,100
Ending Cash*	1,200	900	(300)	(100)

*Ending Cash = Receivables - Payables

Scary but helpful

It's important to realize that while this process can be scary, it's far better for your business's success and survival that you know what today's and the future's snapshots look like. As you get experienced with cash flow forecasting, you will find that even a bad situation today might be over, or improved, in a short while.

Making your forecast also dramatically highlights what some of your most urgent priorities ought to be. If you are worried about a customer's ability to pay a big bill, it's time to take up contact and learn about her own current and future business outlooks. If necessary, you can discuss a change in payment terms to ease pressure on her cash flow but still get some cash in for your own business's needs—if your business can support that. Or if her outlook is grim, you may have to speak next with your banker about some form of interim financing to get you through the coming rough time.

It's not always bad news time when you update your cash flow forecast, however. You may be able to see that in the next six months (if things go as foreseen, of course) you will have paid down your start-up loan. It might be time now to look further ahead and see what that means for your business: time to get a new loan to replace that antique equipment you started with? Time to hire a person to really focus on sales in a new channel? And so forth.

And speaking of bankers, you can understand why they expect you to know how your cash flow is looking. They judge how solid your forecasting skills are, based on your track record. It doesn't help your credibility if you say vaguely that you *think* you can repay your loan on time if X, Y and Z all happen with 100 per-cent certainty—and those things never have happened as hoped before!

If any of this is new to you, it is probably dawning on you that the whole process of cash flow forecasting relies on your having tight control of the data related to your receivables and payables. If you can't locate a bill or a bank state-ment, or you can't tell if your invoicing is up to date, we're sorry, but you're really in a mess. We'll have more to say about this in a moment.

Some internal causes of cash flow problems

As an entrepreneur (unless your business is in the financial sector), you can't be expected to be a specialist in your company's main business focus as well as a top-notch accountant. Sure, you need to grasp all the basics of business finance that apply to you, and be able to talk with bankers, investors, accountants, customers and others with a reasonable degree of intelligence. But as we've said, it's important to know what you don't know, and to seek solid professional sup-port for your internal accounting purposes.

Right from the get-go you should get bookkeeping software and hire some-one with accounting experience to keep track of your books. This person doesn't have to be a fancy financier—just someone with a head for numbers and details and good organizational skills. If you'd rather play it safe, however, hiring an outside bookkeeping service is also an option. Have your bookkeeping person either set up or show you how to set up your internal data systems for accounting purposes. Then it becomes your job to ensure that whoever does your accounting is meticulous in record keeping and reporting. Without accurate, easily accessible data, you are sunk.

You can also run into major cash flow problems due to poor internal com-munications. It is possible that expenses outweigh income, but the books won't reflect the imbalance due to sloppy reporting, internal politics, poor performance by key players, mistakes and the like. This problem can paralyze a company, so keep your radar open for any signs of systematic or human problems that need your intervention.

Believe it or not, delayed or disorganized invoicing is another major source of cash flow problems that many businesses face. You would think that with all the precariousness of a start-up business, getting correct invoices out as soon as possible would be a top priority for everybody. Yet there are times when the work is done, or products are shipped, but it isn't invoiced yet. Every day an invoice is delayed in being sent to your customer risks a later payment than you are due. It will pay off if you periodically sit down with key players in your customer delivery chain to smoke out problems in product or service delivery, invoicing, collecting and so on. It will maintain people's focus on getting those invoices out and provide opportunities to improve processes based on the workers' insights into snags and weaknesses.

And the problem extends to collecting past due invoices as well. If you can believe it, some businesspeople say that they are too busy to chase down outstanding invoices. Use your accounting software to generate daily or weekly ageing reports and ensure that all past due accounts receive reminders.

Slow or low-volume sales can also lead to cash flow problems. Obviously, for a company to make large profits, the sales should be made quickly and in huge numbers. In a case where the company is experiencing slow sales, the amount of income will also tend to be low—makes sense. It may be time to review your marketing strategy and sales practices to boost both dimensions of sales in the future.

External causes of cash flow problems

Of course the state of your economy, the trends in your business sector, international or nature-related events and a host of other forces will impact your cash flow. Since you can't affect most of these factors, the best you can do is try to keep up with news and commentary about them. Cash flow analysis can point to innovative ways you can manage the impact of external forces. For example, if energy costs are rising, would it make sense for you to invest in solar panels for the roof of your office or warehouse? You can chart the outlay to get the panels installed and see how soon energy savings will pay you back.

But not all external forces are huge in scope. You may have a well-oiled invoicing process, but slow-paying customers can still cause serious cash flow problems. Collections can be viewed as an internal matter, but actually making collections is essentially external. It doesn't really matter where you locate it. The solution lies in maintaining frequent contact with slow-paying customers and exploring flexible terms as needed. If you have some cash reserves, that helps ease pressure on you, but the goal is to get every invoice paid on time.

If your cash flow forecasts are looking mostly negative, that obviously tells you that you need to adjust things so your receivables exceed payables. Review sales performance to see if there's any way to increase income. Review expenses to see where you can cut them. Look at additional sources of credit, but don't fool yourself and get too deep into debt if the picture doesn't convince you that you can make a turnaround.

Don't be afraid to ask for help, and update reguarly!

Understanding the Credit Industry

In the good old days, many transactions involving
money were based on trust or faith.
Now, they revolve around credit.

CREDIT GRANTING AND CREDIT USE use have evolved into an entire industry, involving and affecting countless participants from every industry and from every segment of the world's economy. As an entrepreneur, you will certainly need credit, so it's vital to understand how this key success factor works.

Today, credit in some form is required for the economic survival of nearly all consumers and businesses. It's neither intrinsically good or bad—it's how you use it to your advantage that matters.

Credit is simply a measurement of the risk that a creditor, such as a financial institution or a retail store, agrees to grant to its customer. When the risk factor is determined, credit then lets the credit user borrow funds or pay on some schedule of extended terms for a product or service. As a result, the importance credit plays in the economy is nearly immeasurable, and it has become an industry that circulates unimaginable sums of money every day.

The forces of change

The credit industry is directly affected by the local as well as the global environment. External factors such as unemployment rates, the strength of a government's currency against other global economies, and import/export ratios all affect the internal factors of the industry. Some of these internal aspects help set the interest rates creditors can offer, the credit limits and amounts of money available to be lent, and even the requirements for extending the credit itself. One thing is certain: the absolute *uncertainty* of the economy from day to day, and more so from year to year. Forecasters such as economists, financial advisors, and even governmental organizations like the World Bank or the U.S. Federal Reserve

Bank constantly strive for innovative ways to improve upon the accuracy of their predictions of the status of the economy. Unfortunately, an incalculable array of influencing factors makes 100 percent accuracy impossible. The supply and use of credit therefore remains in flux.

For the American consumer, for example, the determining factor of each individual's credit worthiness hinges upon a crucial number. That number is her credit score. This critical number directly establishes the credit worthiness of a consumer, in nearly every instance. Credit scores are determined by the information contained in a consumer's credit file, which in turn is published in a credit report. The higher the score, the better the terms and conditions creditors will be able to offer. Around the world, the reports themselves are usually generated by organizations known as Credit Reporting Agencies. Even in countries where these don't (yet) exist, similar evaluations take place less formally. Creditors don't like to lose money.

In the U.S., Equifax, TransUnion and Experian are the three main players responsible for compiling and storing the data that makes up a consumer credit report. Around the world, other players include Dun & Bradstreet, Experian, Cortera, Credit Information Bureau, Compuscan and CreditInfo. You can Google *credit bureau, consumer reporting agency* or *credit reference agency* for your country's key players.

The data that these companies gather and process includes information received from creditors who supply the monthly results of their customers' payment history. This sequence, through a proprietary scoring system, creates your credit score. In the U.S., nearly every consumer has a credit file and score stored in each of the three credit reporting agency databases. Currently, the average credit score in America stands at approximately 693, out of a possible perfect score of 850, according to Credit.com (http://www.credit.com/press/statistics/credit-report-and-score-statistics.html/).

Companies likewise can be rated according to their credit worthiness. Standard and Poor's, Moody's, Fitch Rating, DBRS and other multinational firms are joined by many country-specific firms in providing this information to lenders and investors. You can find your local players on the Internet.

The impact of an industry

The credit industry links numerous participants in a cyclical structure. The primary suppliers in this industry are the consumers themselves. They fuel the economy through their purchasing power. And when they can't pay in cash, they turn to credit. The secondary supplier then performs its task, with lenders and creditors extending credit to the consumer, thus allowing consumers to purchase goods and services. Creditors charge a fee for their service in the form of interest, which covers profit plus the risk associated with operating on the basis of faith and trust. This process allows for the distribution of goods and services by the manufacturers, service suppliers and retailers. Producing and selling these goods and services creates the movement of the economy as a whole.

But the impact of credit can be seen in other settings as well. Your credit score can determine the interest rate you receive when financing a home, car, or education. It can also determine your credit worthiness as an entrepreneur when you need to finance a new business (or expand an existing one).

Few may realize their credit score can also become involved to the job interview process, the quotes you receive on various types of insurance, and even in a background check for security clearances, etc. In fact, it could be said that a credit score can be the most important number in a person's life today. It follows you everywhere and forever.

With the credit industry spreading its sphere of influence like this, consumers and businesspeople are now facing the task of learning how credit works and what to do to positively affect their personal and business credit reports in order to take advantage of the system in place. Knowledge and education are the keys here. And although the credit industry was formed for an entirely different reason, it has now been officially tasked to help in educating people everywhere, due to the public outcry for information regarding the way credit reports and scores are devised and maintained. In 2003, the United States federal government mandated that all Americans receive a free credit report from each of three reporting agencies each year.

What this means for you as an entrepreneur

You may or may not be inclined to take an interest in credit practices, reports and the like. But both as a private person and an entrepreneur, you cannot afford to neglect your credit profile or to ignore the implications of credit-related decisions you make every day. At a minimum, start with these things (we'll assume here that these apply equally to you privately and in business):

- Order credit reports from the entities that issue them in your location and study them.

- If you spot anything wrong or misleading, contact the issuer and discuss the actions open to you.

- If you find that in fact, you or your business have a poor rating, talk with the issuing agency, your bank, or other reliable sources about how to improve it. It may take a lot longer to improve your rating than it took to get into trouble. But you owe it to yourself or business to raise your score—because you'll pay for the lower one in higher costs of borrowing until it does rise.

- If you live in a place that doesn't have such credit rating agencies, use your trusted connections to find out how you or your company are viewed financially. If you hear concerns, get help in addressing them.

- Make a practice of running credit checks on yourself and your business as part of your annual planning cycle.

- Keep an eye on changes in credit conditions and laws that may bear on you. If you have complex credit needs, it may be smart to hire an independent advisor to monitor and report these to you periodically (especially if it's not your true passion or you don't have the time).

Change continues

One thing is certain: the credit industry will continue to change as the landscape of every economy across the globe and their dependency on alternatives to cash and bartering fluctuates. New and innovative lending and credit practices will continue to change the face of the credit industry and its impact on us all. That's why you need to watch out for changes that could affect your ability to borrow money, open or expand businesses, negotiate interest rates, and so forth. Make it your goal to become a minimal credit risk to your financing partners and they will be glad to work with you to help fund the goods, services and capital you need to thrive in your personal and business life.

Your Credit Report and Scores

*We've accomplished the first step in understanding
how the credit industry has evolved and how it
currently plays a major role in every economy
around the world. What's next?*

DRILLING DOWN FURTHER in the credit landscape, let's look now at how individual credit reports, and ultimately the corresponding credit scores, are examined by creditors and lending organizations around the world to determine an individual or company's level of credit worthiness. Simply put, analysis of the score will ultimately determine if a person or business has the qualifications to receive favorable financing they seek to buy the goods or services they need.

Let's start with the basics. A credit report is a record of your financial behavior and performance over time. It consists of categorized information about your credit-related activities and reveals how responsibly you have used particular credit resources, and subsequently, fulfilled your financial commitments. An individual or business develops a credit history that commences with individual creditors and broadens over time, until it is ultimately collected and evaluated by the credit reporting agencies around the world.

The credit reporting industry is a sophisticated network of lenders, creditors, merchants, and similar sources. They furnish creditors with credit data to on the consumers and businesses that are applying for and using credit. So a credit reporting agency's main purpose is to supply risk management data to creditors. Equally, lending organizations, such as banks and financing companies, are required to manage risk. Credit reporting agencies also help those organizations do this by providing them with information they can use to assess a particular borrower.

Score big... and win!

After all of this information is compiled, most credit reporting agencies assign corresponding ratings or scores to the history-packed reports. Those scores are calculated using multiple factors. They can be the first thing a creditor views when making decisions on extending credit to the proposed borrower. So, the more you know about *how* your credit score is calculated, the easier it will be for you to sustain a good one. The key is remembering one thing: The higher your score, the lower the risk you pose to a creditor.

Credit score calculations usually follow roughly the same pattern in every credit reporting agency. These factors can include payment history, amount of debt owed, age of credit, the different mixes of credit, and even recent credit applications (or credit inquiries). In most cases (and certainly in the United States) each of these factors can be weighted. Make sure you are familiar with this process wherever you are seeking credit. For example, in the United States, an individual's payment history and the amount owed to creditors make up 65 percent of her credit score. Here are a few tips that can help you maintain a high quality credit score.

- **Pay your bills on time.** Being late on a payment isn't good for your score. Missing a payment can compound into even more problems. A good rule is to pay early... and pay the bill in full if possible.

- **Keep those credit card balances low.** It's not a good idea to have any significant balances for any reason on credit cards. This is how financial responsibility is earned... or lost. The amount of debt you have in comparison to your credit limits is known as credit utilization. If you have a balance on a credit card (or on more than one), keep it low. The higher your credit utilization, the lower your score will be. Keep the utilization of all cards to 30 percent or less.

- **Monitor and manage your overall debt**. Even if you have a satisfactory payment history on your debt, too much of it can also hurt your score. Keeping a solid debt-to-credit ratio is crucial in maintaining a solid score.

- **Keep old credit cards open:** Believe it or not, even when you close a credit card it can hurt your credit score. If your credit card issuer stops sending monthly updates to the credit bureaus (even if the account has no balance), your score could be compromised. Your credit history with that creditor will also cease. Additionally, if the credit available is suddenly closed on that account, your overall debt-to-credit ratios will be negatively affected.

- **Be careful of making too many credit inquiries:** Every time you apply for new credit, your score stands to take a temporary small hit. Also, opening a new credit account can lower your score, because your average credit age is negatively affected. Seek new credit accounts sparingly to avoid a drop in score.

The good old days

The manner in which consumers apply for loans, both business or personal, has changed dramatically in the last several decades. Do you remember your parents or even grandparents ever telling you about how they used to do business with a bank or finance company? I do. The story seemed so simple, mostly because it *was* simple, back in those days.

When I was much younger (and well before I ever started my first business), my grandfather explained exactly how he did business with the local bank in his community. He described the ease with which he was able to walk into the bank, without an appointment, and to speak directly to the bank manager, who was the sole decision-maker for most financial transactions the bank made locally. His relationship with that bank manager was relaxed and slow paced. The bank manager, of course, lived in the same community.

Because he did all of his banking business there (his personal accounts, loans, etc. as well as business finance), the two of them were able to discuss the new, proposed loan or extension of credit with very little paperwork or red tape. The reason was simple: The bank manager had a personal history with my grandfather. They both knew each other's character. The banker trusted Grandpa and my grandfather reciprocated. Incredibly, he told other stories about the bank manager actually stopping by his home on occasion to see how things were going. After all, they were both members of the local community.

In fact, a quick look at his previous business dealings with the bank, a short discussion, a review of his the current situation and personal news, and some additional paperwork was about all it took for the deal to go through. And although his transactions may have never been on a major scale, the process of completing the financial transactions were as stress-free as you can imagine. A single one-on-one, realistic discussion was all that was needed to figure out the credit situation and construct the new stage. That was how it used to be done. That was then.

Today, you're just a number

We would all like to think we have connections. Inside links at the bank or any other financial institution are obviously beneficial. However, your biggest asset will always be what's hidden in your credit scores. In today's financial landscape, credit score management has become the most important single factor in getting credit for your small business or yourself. In fact, you could say that credit scores have almost become a form of currency, due to the way they are weighed by the creditors themselves.

Data can be transmitted around the world in seconds now. We can acquire loans and financing in distant cities or countries when the need arises. Our investigations for financing and credit may involve Internet searches and reports from any corner of the globe. We may never even meet the person giving us a loan or step foot into that lending institution for the transaction, either. Reports, scores and other supporting info can be amalgamated in an instant; and credit worthiness can be determined on a computer screen. This is how it's done today.

So understanding your personal credit reports is where it all begins. Knowing what will affect your corresponding scores is just as vital. This gives you a major advantage in the credit-using world. Empower yourself through education and research and give yourself a huge dose of self-discipline until you can deliver the rock-solid credit reporting and scoring information that your creditors want to see. This way, you can use your understanding of the new landscape and take advantage of it. You can make yourself a perfect candidate for the best interest rates and get quick approvals for the loans, credit and financing you need for *your* business.

M.P.

Getting Your Financial House in Order

*The title above seems simple and straightforward. However, these
few words can have immeasurable significance in your life.*

REGARDLESS OF WHETHER you are starting a new business, expanding your
existing company, or just wanting more financial stability in your personal life, a
quick review of how you are structuring and storing relevant financial documentation is a perfect place to start.

Knowing where your information is stored, how it is filed and in what
format you keep it is basic prudence. Nevertheless, not all of us are that prudent.
Getting—and staying—organized in general is not only a good idea in order to
maximize success in your life, it is vital. The most important thing is to be set
up so that if you or someone in your household or business needs to find some
documentation, it can be located immediately.

Let's get organized

First, let's take a look at your private financial data management. Being able
to get your hands on essential paperwork such as your mortgage contracts, deeds,
insurance policies, vehicle information, health and medical records, credit and
loan statements, and similar documentation is crucial. And it's an ongoing battle,
because we all have an incredible amount of data being thrown at us via countless
communications each month.

Checking to see if there are changes to your accounts and their policies, validating charges, reconciling your monthly books, and even inspecting every document for inaccuracies is an absolute must, especially in this era of identity theft
and Internet scams. Empowering yourself to be in-the-know about everything
being reported about you and the records that will be archived for future use is
imperative. For these reasons, we recommend that you have your credit report(s)
and score(s) pulled once per quarter, to catch and correct possible factual errors.

But what should you do about your business documentation? The same
scenario applies here too. In the following paragraphs, we're going to go over a

few basics to apply. Keep in mind that no matter whether your small business is already off the ground or if you are simply interested in getting organized for a future launch, having a structured portfolio of documents that may eventually be needed by a bank or lending institution is central to navigating the waters of financing and credit applications. Depending on the nature of your business type or the length of your current or proposed business history, here is a brief sampling of possible documentation (personal and/or business-related) that may be required to be organized, accurate and up to date.

- Bank statements
- Tax returns
- Legal filings, including contracts, permits, and so forth
- Business plans
- Marketing plans
- Strategic plans
- Profit and loss statements
- Budgets
- Expense sheets
- Lists of assets
- Lists of collateral
- Personal financials
- Letters of reference
- Accounting ledgers
- Insurance documents
- Credit card statements and account numbers
- Medical records and contact information as needed
- Property-related documents
- Up-to-date licensing agreements for future tax purposes, loan applications, and credit extensions from lenders and creditors

One step at a time

Even before your business is off the ground, it is absolutely necessary for you to develop a comprehensive system of organized record-keeping. This practice will enable your business to slowly transition out of that need to supply personal documentation until you can present company-based documentation to any entities requiring it. Of course, your system may not be perfect at first, but a really tight, logical system should be your goal, no matter how small and simple your business is. With time you may need professional accounting services, but at first you may be able to do it all yourself. (Ideally, if you can learn from such professionals how they would organize things before you set them up, you'll be ahead of the game.)

So organizing your documents and records today will help you be prepared for any future needs for information. It will also be central in protecting your identity, providing security, and keeping you on track for accurate planning overall. Here are a few initial pointers on getting your financial house in order.

- **Generate a master list of your necessary documents.** Using the information already provided in this section (and in connection with the files and accounts you currently uphold) create a working roster of vital documents to organize and maintain. There is no better place to begin this overall process than making this essential master list.

- **Maintain accurate and up-to-date records... always.** It's been mentioned a few times but bears repeating here. You must take charge of ensuring the accuracy on every document. One error on a crucial document could alter your entire loan application standing or even affect future interest rate changes on revolving accounts. Maintain a complete and chronological list of all statements. Make sure to file every statement (monthly or quarterly) too. Lenders will not allow gaps in record-keeping. Finally, be mindful of the expiration date(s) on credit cards, insurances and warranties. Know the renewal dates for everything and be proactive about renewing, if applicable.

- **Develop security measures for your protection.** Nearly every statement you receive from the companies handling your accounts contains personal and/or financial information that could expose you to fraud or even identity theft. Take measures to secure all documents in a safe place that provides access to only those needing that information (family members, business associates, etc.). Consider making a password-protected master list of passwords, user IDs, and similar sensitive information and do *not* print it out. Additionally, store duplicate copies of key documents (hard copies or digital ones) offsite to preserve them against fire, flood or other natural disasters. A safety deposit box at the bank branch in which you have accounts is always a good place for back-up copies. A rule of thumb is to back up as often as necessary so you can afford to lose what hasn't been backed up yet—which means often!

- **Preserve tax returns and records.** Every country has different requirements here. You should be aware of how many years' worth of records you need to store for future use. Tax authorities have a right to audit you without notice in most places. Be prepared with your documents and supporting evidence at all times. Some of these records may also be required by lenders for verification purposes regarding a loan you may be seeking for your small business. Keep a master copy of multiple years' returns and then make a back-up for emergency purposes as well.

- **Review, update and stay relevant.** Organizing your financials is essential and keeping on top of it is equally so for both your personal and business financials. Once to twice a year, review your business, financial, marketing and strategic plans to make sure they are still relevant. If things have changed (personal situations, market conditions, economy, pricing, budgets, etc.), those items need to be reflected in your various plans. Lenders and funding organizations will need current and accurate information to be able to properly review and underwrite a loan proposal for you. This practice is also essential if you are seeking outside investors or business partners.

- **Safely dispose of unnecessary documents.** If old, out-of-date or irrelevant documents are no longer needed, take care to dispose of them properly. Shredding is a must for paper documents. If you find those document piles are getting big, there are professional document destruction companies that can assist you in disposing of your paperwork safely and securely. Similarly, you can buy software that can ensure computer files you don't want to save are eliminated. Do not neglect this responsibility.

- **Make this a habit.** All the tips and practices above can seem daunting, but you need to take them just as seriously as you take on loan obligations or hire a new person for your business. Your credibility and credit worthiness rest on your command and protection of these essentials to your personal and business life.

Your house is now in order—now what?

Getting your financial house in order may seem like a small step in the overall process of successful starting and running a small business. But it gives you a solid foundation to grow on. And it will also create a huge stepping stone in developing and managing your relationships with future lenders. We'll have more to say on this in later sections.

Finding and Working with the Right Accountant

The money you spend on getting sound financial services in some ways may be the best investment you'll make when you start a business.

POOR BUSINESS ACCOUNTING or tax planning can easily derail development of a great business idea or concept. A qualified professional resource is key to optimizing the financial success of your business.

Not a do-it-yourself project

A common mistake entrepreneurs make when starting a business is to save money by setting up their accounting system themselves, using widely available accounting programs like QuickBooks *without professional guidance*. The basic bookkeeping and daily accounting functions may be easy to execute. It may even be relatively easy to set up the various charts of accounts. Someone with a good background in finance may be comfortable setting up such accounting programs, assigning cost centers and implementing day-to-day business accounting. The challenge is in setting up the most appropriate cost centers, organizing appropriate depreciation schedules, knowing what to treat as one-time expenses or amortized expenses, and other specifics related to tax planning or effective business accounting.

Leading tax accounting professionals we have worked with while reviewing various businesses we have considered buying or investing in have often found errors in the way businesses have set up their charts of accounts. They spot errors in accounting entries, and missed opportunities in tax planning. The first mistake is often related to setting up depreciation schedules (depreciation means taking down the value of something over a scheduled period of time, like three years, or spreading its cost over its expected lifetime). By setting up one depreciation schedule for tax reporting and another one for business accounting, you can optimize the benefits attributable to each. For example, for tax reporting purposes it may be helpful to use a more accelerated depreciation schedule to create more deductible offsets to income tax obligations. This would be a good strategy for a business where principles are interested in maximizing tax deductions earlier. Of course, if your tax planning requires few or no deductions early on, a long-term depreciation schedule could be implemented. The point is that it takes a specialist to grasp the larger implications of choices you make in your bookkeeping and tax preparations. It's far better to have that specialist make a recommendation and back it up with explanations that to take a shot in the dark all by yourself—and miss.

One accountant or two?

Depreciation schedules are only one example of the need for professional guidance in your financial planning. Tax laws and requirements vary by location and often change more frequently than the average business owner can comfortably track. There are a number of elements a good tax accountant organizes and monitors to optimize the tax planning for a business.

Effective business accounting requires more than just tax planning, however. Business accounting practices need to balance with a solid tax planning strategy to achieve the best possible outcome for the financial success of your business. What many business owners mistake in the selection of their professional accounting resources are the difference in skills and capabilities needed for tax accountants and business accountants. Often a good business accountant is not as effective in tax planning and preparation. In many cases the good tax accountant is not as effective in daily business accounting processes. Finding and working with the right accountant starts with a very important question. Is there one professional resource available to provide the most effective tax and business accounting service, or do you need to look separately for a qualified tax professional and a qualified business accountant?

The selection process

The process of selecting the right accountant or accountants begins with preparing a list of candidates and developing an effective interview strategy.

Where can you find candidates? Start by asking other small business owners who they work with and find out what they think the plusses and minuses of their choices are. Your banker might be willing to recommend some accountants too. If you have worked with a personal tax planner before, you might already have a candidate for at least your business's tax accounting. There are of course directories, professional associations, and small business development agencies that can broaden your list if you want.

There are four categories to consider when interviewing professional accounting resources for your business.

- Tax planning and preparation
- Business accounting practices
- Fundamental understanding of your business
- Clearly understandable pricing or fee schedule

Prepare number of questions that will help define the quality and fit of the professional resource you are interviewing. Here are some questions that will be effective for the interview process.

1. What are the most important elements related to proper tax planning for my business, short and medium term?

2. What is your process for identifying and setting up the proper chart of accounts for my business accounting?

3. Which accounting software do you recommend for my business?

4. What are the key items I should track daily or weekly in my business?

5. What is the best strategy for depreciation for both business accounting and tax planning?

6. Do you have any clients with a business similar to mine that I may speak with, as one of your references?

7. Do you have a professional fee schedule or hourly rate in writing for me to review?

8. How long has your firm been in business, and how long have you been an associate?

9. How many business clients does your firm represent? How many do you represent?

10. What are your business credentials, degrees, and/or certificates?

11. Do you mostly do business accounting or tax accounting?

Add extra questions to test your candidates' general knowledge about your specific business and the specific locations in which you operate. For example, if you do international business, probe for experience and training in that regard.

After completing an interview process you will have a much better understanding and expectation about the capabilities of the accountant and his or her potential fit with your business. You may learn that you want to work with one resource for both tax accounting and business accounting or you may determine it works better to select one for business accounting and a separate accountant for tax services.

Ongoing work with your accountant

Finding the right accountant is important, but working with the accountant on an ongoing basis is key to the successful development of your business. Too often a business owner does not coordinate with her accountant to monitor and manage the key drivers of the financial success of the business. Your accountant may be very helpful in identifying the most important measurements to monitor on a daily or weekly basis to keep pace with your business planning and financial goals. To maximize your financial results, work with your accountant to develop a specific list of what will be monitored and how you will respond to variations in expected performance. Following a clear plan, tracking key information, and responding timely to variances will optimize the performance of your business.

Managing Your Relationship with Your Lender

It's not where you start… but where you finish.
Communicate and win!

YOU ARE READY TO SELECT a bank for your new business. Now what?

Obviously, you thought about the bank's location, hours and array of services. Those were the very basics, based on your own research or even a colleague's referral. But what about the next level of factors that need to be addressed?

Often, entrepreneurs fail to dig a little deeper to learn about the how a bank interacts with its small business banking and lending customers. They may never even interview a bank officer about lending practices, decision-making on check-clearing processes, or the bank's track record of success with other small businesses in the area. It is vital to consider these additional aspects before selecting a bank for your small business needs. So if you haven't made the final choice yet, or even if you have, consider the following advice.

It's not where you start… but where you finish

Initially, your small business may need nothing more than having the bank handle your deposits, withdrawals and debit cards. Without question, this can be a good foundation for a banking relationship. However, developing a *successful* banking relationship goes well beyond these narrow parameters. In fact, when developed, and then later managed well, a banking relationship can really help a company thrive and grow over the years.

And thinking of the future, there is often a natural progression in banking relationships. Small businesses that grow into large-scale corporations may at some point decide it's in their best interest to use more than one bank. This may be for many reasons. You may want to have two or more banks presenting competitive proposals for the financial services you need. Or you have a very long personal history and therefore a stronger trust base with one, yet another is hungry for new customers. One may have a unique service that another lacks. The "feel" of one bank may or may not suit you, despite its competitive terms or good service, etc. The important thing to remember, however, is that if you deal with more than one bank, your business will then need to manage multiple banking relationships. And that will require time and attention.

Once your business becomes even larger, it may be necessary to create additional relationships with investment banks as well. Investment banks support individuals, corporations and even governments with various services such as foreign exchange transactions, mergers and acquisitions, mutual funds, hedge funds and pension funds. Regardless of your needs, the scale of your business or the timeline involved, creating and then managing your relationship with your bank(s) can be as significant as any other aspect of business on your path to success.

Communicate... and win!

Research indicates that a large percentage of business owners feel trepidation regarding their banker(s) and, as a result, experience a disconnect when interacting with them. You should never let this happen. Your bankers, if vetted properly for a perfect fit, will be key players in your financial dealings. And if your communication with them meets their expectations and requirements, they should see you as a partner as well. To say communication is important is a complete understatement.

There are really two keys to banking relationship success: communication and time. Spending quality time and communicating professionally and candidly with your banker, especially in the early stages of developing a relationship, works to establish a better understanding, trust and working knowledge of your organization's operations, inside and out. Be prepared to educate your banker about the key factors in your business—a good banker is business savvy, but may not have worked with customers in your particular sector before. This fundamental process of sharing will also stabilize and reinforce the view your banker has developed about you, both personally and as a business person.

Meeting with your banker once a year or only when a problem arises just doesn't cut it. If your company has just won an award or secured a big contract, make sure your banker knows about it. And if you've set sales records, added more clients or even been featured in the local paper, include your banker in your public relations announcement list too. This reinforcement helps the banker get a feeling of where you fit in your marketplace, compared with your competition. It can pay off in a future loan or credit line process down the road. This sort of information is difficult to translate onto an application; it's all the more reason to keep positive lines of communication open.

Make time

We mentioned time as a key relationship factor above. As with any relationship, you need to invest time to foster its growth. Like all entrepreneurs, you wear many hats, and the finance one may not fit your head as well as some of the others on your rack. However, the benefits of a strong relationship with your bank always reward the time you invest in it. You and your banker should review your bank statements, financials and other important documents together a few times a year so both sides understand each other.

Time is important here in another sense. Recognize that you will need adequate time to be thorough and organized in your financial dealings. When it does come time for that application for credit or loan, taking as much time as you need to do it right is an absolute must. This includes providing the bank with every piece of documentation requested, no matter how trivial it may seem to you. Yes, this takes time and effort. But once again, taking great care will make your professionalism shine through, and that will pay off, regardless of the banking goals you may have.

What happens if things don't go as planned for your business? Taking the time to clearly and neutrally communicate bad news is just as important as sharing the positives. Both you and your banker are striving for an overall body of work that tells a story over time. This is a fundamental reason for staying in touch and providing both positive and negative news, plus information and documentation that concern your business. You can be sure that your banker will love this open line of communication. Why? Bankers hate surprises… except if they are jam-packed with great news.

The lesson here is simple: Take the time to establish a trusting relationship with the best possible banker you can find to fit your banking and lending needs. Grow that relationship by communicating effectively and by providing everything the banker needs to make educated decisions about helping you grow your business. Working closely together as a team will increase the odds of financial success for both you and the bank.

Tools and Resources

*There is a wealth of help for entrepreneurs who want
or need support and encouragement!*

IT CAN BE LONELY and even scary at times when you are starting a business
and have to confront an ocean of financial decisions simultaneously. Sometimes,
even just having a comrade to share successes and disappointments with, ask for
advice, or bounce ideas around with is a big help. And there are lots of other tools
and resources out there too.

The business press. You may already have the habit of skimming business
pages, magazines, books and blogs, and if so, you know that you can learn a lot
about business and finance from the experiences of others. In fact, suddenly these
publications take on a lot more importance once you start thinking of yourself as
an entrepreneur. Even the biggest companies were start-ups at one time, so you
have lots of real-life lessons to learn from them.

Social media. Of course you have to protect your time and privacy, given
all you are trying to do every day, but you might identify people you connect with
who offer real-time, useful help and answers.

Networking. If you're going nuts in your tiny home office, or feel lonely
at the top, it can be a refreshing break and a source for new contacts and ideas if
you try attending various events that make sense for your business. Keep an open
mind about the focus of the group; it may not be strictly tied to your business's
specifics (e.g., it could be a city hall meeting about a new plan that reroutes traffic
and could affect your walk-in business, for example). The benefits of circulating
and developing new connections are many. Consider joining a Chamber of Commerce, Rotary or Kiwanis group. Even donating some time toward a good cause
can have unexpected business benefits besides doing good.

Mentors. You may find that a small business support agency in your area sponsors "loaned executives" or volunteer retirees who agree to adopt a small business founder, meet regularly to see how things are progressing and give advice or feedback. Mentors don't have to be older than you, either. You could also join or start a Mastermind group. These groups are listed on the Internet, along with information on how to form your own group. They meet regularly and share plans, successes, and failures under structured discussion formats. You can learn a lot, and who knows, you may know something that can help another entrepreneur to succeed. That can feel great.

Courses. There are excellent courses, both live and online, to help you improve your business skills, and finance is one big focus here (starting perhaps with Accounting for Non-Financial Managers?). Night classes, one-shot training events, and so forth can really pay off in your command of your finances.

Efficiency tools. We include software (certainly Excel and QuickBooks come to mind), time management books or workshops, and even office equipment and supplies that just make your work life simpler in this category. As we've mentioned, accounting software like QuickBooks can be a boon to small businesses, but it's best to ask your accountant to set up your company on it if you decide to use it. And don't forget to ask other businesspeople what their favorite apps are for their work.

Incubator office set-ups. In addition to providing a menu of services like telephone answering, copying and scanning facilities, meeting rooms, office space and so forth, these facilities naturally attract entrepreneurs and often, very innovative thinkers of all stripes. There's a natural community in them and that can open doors and provide you with fresh insights. Chances are your office neighbors won't know your business, so they may have original perspectives on problems you are wrestling with.

With so much potential support out there, don't feel obliged to follow up on any of these tips unless they feel right for you. Your business is your main job, after all. But you never know, it might just go better if you get one good idea....

Your Business Plan: An Overview*

It's important to see how your financial plans fit with the rest of your business planning.

AS YOU ALREADY have seen, a sound business plan is critical to your financial success as an entrepreneur. Preparing it frankly requires a lot of work, but the exercise repays you by reducing the number of things that can surprise you, shining light on aspects of your intentions, plans or resources that are shaky, and developing your confidence that you've done your homework and are ready for the big test.

Of course, your plan will reflect the level of complexity and scope of the business you are starting. But even if you are simply opening a hotdog stand, it pays to think through all the applicable parts and have clearly stated, written answers worked out. That stand may become the next big hot dog chain! And you will find that supplying the expected information will sharpen your own vision and give you a greater sense of ownership in the business you are starting.

So the first and most important reader of your business plan is *you*. You will probably go back to this document again and again as you move forward. Consider it a changeable road map. But your plan also may be read by potential partners, banks, investors, key hires, organizations which grant subsidies, and so forth. Below are the key elements. You can find a more detailed discussion of each of them in the Appendix.

The EXECUTIVE SUMMARY is a brief paragraph that describes your company and its industry sector. Include any industry standards and statistics that support your reasons for expecting your business's success. If you are adapting your plan for a funding request, at the start of this paragraph, clearly state the total capital requirements requested of the reader (investor, bank, etc.).

*This section first appeared in our book *A Crash Course in Starting a Business* (Nova Vista Publishing, ISBN 978-90-77256-36-7).

The MARKET ANALYSIS portion is a detailed profile of your target market and its consumers. The more *relevant* data you can gather to support your claim that your target market is in need of your new product or business, the better.

In the COMPANY DESCRIPTION portion, provide the reader with an understanding of your company's business structure, e.g., corporation, limited liability company, sole proprietorship. Also include your mission statement, continuing with a sentence or two that details the planned direction of the organization for the next few years. Close this section with the most current mailing address and contact information of the business and key players.

Create an ORGANIZATION AND MANAGEMENT section, introducing the reader to the founders and other noteworthy participants in the business. Provide a detailed description of the persons listed above, explaining their titles, involvement, experience, qualifications and pertinent supplementary information. If your business includes more than one level of participants, an organization chart would be useful.

In the MARKETING AND SALES STRATEGY section, the first thing you want to do is define your marketing strategy. There is no single way to approach a marketing strategy. However, there are common steps you can follow to help you think through the direction and tactics you plan to use to go to market, drive sales and sustain customer loyalty.

An overall marketing strategy should include, at a minimum, four separate strategy statements for your market penetration, growth, distribution, and communication.

Include any pertinent demographic research and industry trends and profiles. Touch on the different market segments you plan to sell to, and how you plan to approach them. Include plans as needed for appropriate local, regional, national, international and web-based marketing. If a website is in the plan, this is where you should outline its development, including consumer imagery, functionality and search engine optimization (SEO). Discuss the media you will use, including back-up plans in case revenues can't fund all the activity you plan. Then separately discuss the different marketing and advertising campaigns you plan within each type of media.

Next, define your sales strategy: how you plan to actually sell your products or services. Include two primary elements: your sales force strategy and your sales activities.

In the SERVICE OR PRODUCT LINE section, introduce the reader to your key products or services. Lay out the idea behind each, and detail what makes it a value to your potential customers. Also, explain why yours are better than products or services offered by the competition. Follow this introduction with individual breakdowns of each product or service, if you plan multiple offerings.

In the FUNDING REQUEST section, if that's what you are using this version for, take this opportunity to educate your reader on the direction your team plans to take the business, how much it will cost to get there, and how you will use the funding you are requesting. Make this section read like an internal document, similar to an employee handbook. Give a synopsis of future sales expectations, expansion of the marketing plan, and employee growth. This is where well thought-out ideas regarding streamlining production, promotion and distribution are presented (consider outsourcing, private labeling, licensing, trade marking, and franchising).

The final section, FINANCIALS, is the most crucial to the success of your new business. Create this document to ensure you have done the appropriate research and financial planning to start and operate your business. Include all fixed and variable expenses, then match these numbers with all expected revenue sources. After producing a narrative summary of these items, you will need to prepare the necessary expense reports, including balance sheets, income statements (or forecasts), statements (or forecasts) of cash flow, and pro forma income statements.

Remember, too, that you should include a private placement disclaimer with your business plan if you plan to use it to raise capital. Private placement is the sale of securities directly to an institutional investor, such as a bank, mutual fund, foundation, insurance company, etc. In the U.S., it does not require Securities Exchange Commission (SEC) registration, provided that the securities are purchased for investment purchases only, not for resale. The private placement disclaimer specifies this fact.

Following the Financials section, you may need to include an APPENDIX. It can contain relevant back-up documents like agreements, reports, résumés, and the like.

All copies of your business plan should be controlled, so ensure that you keep a distribution record. This will allow you to update and maintain your business plan on an as-needed basis.

The Financing Section in Your Business Plan

Get this right and you'll have much higher odds of survival—and even success.

AN EFFECTIVE BUSINESS PLAN includes information about all elements of the business and how it will be developed. One of the most critical elements of the business plan is the Financing section. (See additional comments on the Financing section in the Appendix.)

We often hear that nothing happens in business until something is sold. Before that happens, it is the financing that provides the resources to fund the establishment of the business and the initial sales activity. Sadly, all too often, businesses start up with unrealistically limited financial resources, and with the expectation that early and growing sales will provide the funding to carry and grow the business.

We have seen far too many start-ups and younger businesses that lack sufficient funding resources or alternatives. This can lead to the early failure of an otherwise promising-looking emerging business. It is vitally important that the Financing section of your business plan goes well beyond basic spreadsheets of sales revenue projections and corresponding expense targets. Developing these projections is often the primary focus of the Financing section, and they do have to be accurate and well thought out. The key to a really effective Financing section is a well-defined and comprehensive *funding plan* that considers and anticipates all appropriate contingencies.

First you must carefully determine the capital requirements to set up the initial business and fund its operations until its financial performance can sustain the ongoing business. Once your capital requirements have been thoroughly defined, the next step is to identify specific thresholds in your business development timeline when capital needs to be provided. This process will establish your complete capital funding requirements and the timing for use of those funds. Then, the next step is to prepare a well-defined plan for securing capital funding, including secondary sources that could be tapped in the event your primary sources fall short of your expectations or additional funds are needed.

Some typical examples of components used in the Financing section of your business plan may include the following:

- The Primary Funding Source for initial business capital. You should include only funds that are confirmed to be available for the business.

- The Secondary Funding Sources. This should include each source for additional funds and the specific steps that are planned to secure those funds. This section should have multiple methods and/or sources for secondary funding.

- Methods for Funding. This section will outline the details about various funding methods to be pursued and when and how each will be used. Examples include conventional bank financing, venture capital firms, private funding from high-net-worth individuals, private equity, and crowd funding.

- The Variance Plan for funding shortfalls. This segment will have a specific action plan for reducing expenses in the event revenue is below plan and/or funding falls short of plan.

The enthusiasm an entrepreneur puts into the business plan speaks to the fundamentals about the business, how sales will be developed, and the ongoing operations. Too many times this spirited vision blurs an entrepreneur's view of the funding requirements she needs to successfully launch and build the business. Don't risk your early failure by underestimating funding needs or not considering "what-ifs" that won't go away by being ignored.

Always remember that funding is the fuel that drives the plans and initiatives you developed to grow your business. Sales revenue may come slower than expected, and maintaining the momentum on all the sales and marketing programs that drive this growth is critical to the success of your business. Develop an effective and thorough financial plan so that you have the resources to fuel the growth of your business and reach your goals.

CHAPTER II
Methods of Financing

Acquiring Financing or Funding

*Even the simplest businesses cost money. But it comes
in many forms, with many implications
for you as an entrepreneur.*

THERE ARE MANY DIFFERENT ways to acquire financing, so all the preparation and research you do will pay off well. Before searching for financing, it is a good idea to see what grants and subsidies you might qualify for. They could keep you from incurring debt or losing ownership of your business. However, if you don't find such funding available, a variety of other sources of financing can help you get your new business off the ground.

When determining what type of financing to procure for your business, there are many avenues to consider. The type of business you have, your future plans, and the product(s) and service(s) you offer all influence your evaluations of options here, and making a good choice is important. There are two main types of financing: debt or equity. *Debt financing* is the process by which a firm borrows capital (money) from banks and investors, promising to repay the borrowed funds within a certain amount of time with some profit for the lender, usually in the form of interest. The other type is *equity financing*, when a business relinquishes part of its ownership interest to different sources in exchange for capital. Most well-capitalized, established businesses use a balance of both. This helps mitigate risk and keep the cost of capital to a minimum.

Debt financing is usually done by businesses that have either established positive cash flow (money remaining after collecting revenue and paying operating expenses plus any mortgage payments) or have the necessary collateral (equipment, cash or an individual's promissory note) to secure the funds from a lender. When businesses choose this method, they are obliged to pay a carrying cost on the funds. This form of financing is common in two types of businesses. One type deals in high-volume inventory purchases that are later liquidated through sales channels. They get in cash relatively quickly, and thus can keep the term of the loan to a minimum. The other type needs to expand by purchasing space or equipment with a liquidation value similar to the debt they take on (for example, real estate, long-term-use equipment, and vehicles).

Equity financing is something else. It can be a great tool when expanding your firm beyond the size and scope of what you could fund with conventional debt financing. In equity financing, you effectively sell an interest in your company in exchange for funding that is provided by a partner or investor. That way, you can raise needed capital, while only being exposed to a few key liabilities like rent or mortgage, equipment expenses, and employee salaries. (For more on equity compared to debt financing, see pages 73-74).

In order to avoid takeovers or buyouts by these parties, you need to consider who holds the controlling interest in an equity deal. Whoever owns more than 50 percent, the majority percentage of the company's shares, gets to call the shots. Also, depending on the way in which the interest is conveyed, individuals can recoup their investment through multiple channels. This is when contracts detailing cash capital disbursements (debt repayment and/or interest payment) are important.

Here's an example of a vital cash capital disbursement decision. Imagine you accepted a large start-up loan from an investor to get your business off the ground. What does your cash capital disbursement contract say about your repayment terms? Specifically, when you have to pay it back? Do you have to start repaying the loan immediately, or after three to five years? It makes a pretty big difference.

If you have to start paying back the loan immediately, the principal (original amount) plus interest will put a pretty big dent in your allocated operating budget, from Day 1. Is the loan even worth it, at this point? You can see why your cash capital disbursement terms are extremely important. Make sure the financial terms to which you agree are feasible for your business even under a worst-case scenario for the future.

Lastly, remember that there is a strong correlation between risk and reward in funding. If you have to relinquish a good portion of your ownership interest to other investors in order to get the money you need, you may only be entitled to a small portion of the profits, in the event that the business performs extremely well.

There are many different types of private investors and investment groups. The most common is the *accredited investor*. These individuals are familiar with the investment world and have probably participated in such ventures previously. They also have certain qualifications to make them attractive financiers. Another type is an *angel investor*, an individual who has the funds to almost entirely fund the start-up, expansion or growth of a business. Both accredited investors and angel investors are private parties who are not usually affiliated with an investment group.

Investment groups and IPOs

Investment groups, such as *venture capitalists* (VCs), are another option. Venture capital groups are great for companies that are interested in retaining brain-trust equity and/or a portion of the control, but not all. These groups tend to know exactly what they are looking for in exchange for their involvement. The right to controlling interest and substantial portions of revenue is not uncommon. However, by using such groups, a business's current owners can nearly eliminate their personal financial risk. Because the VCs have a sizeable vested interest, expect the participation of seasoned business consultants who will take a hands-on approach and work with your firm to achieve success.

Some entrepreneurial businesses have the ability to approach the public through an *initial public offering* (IPO) of shares of stock. This is the process by which a company works with investment bankers to build a following in a specific trading platform (e.g., a stock exchange), then offers shares representing interest in the company on its behalf, in exchange for a portion of the proceeds. Usually a company has to have a proven track record to launch an IPO, so don't waste time dreaming about IPOs in your early start-up days unless others with experience confirm it's worth considering.

There can be great benefits as well as liabilities associated with making an initial public offering. The most common advantage is that, on average, a firm can collect ten times its value in one offering. In special circumstances, when either the product or service is groundbreaking or there is a large emotional following in the market, an organization can raise exponentially more. This happened frequently during the dot-com era, back in the late Nineties, when technology companies were making IPOs and the stock prices were driven up to staggering multiples above the companies' book value, simply because of investors' speculation on the potential for future success.

Local, regional, or even national governments often provide funding for entrepreneurs, as the Small Business Administration (SBA) does in the U.S. Especially for new businesses, the SBA and similar organizations offer competitive loans, grants and subsidies. However, the majority of these funds are only released to businesses or individuals with specific profiles, such as minorities, persons with disabilities, and individuals coming from a disadvantaged socioeconomic background. If you qualify for this avenue for funding, you will encounter numerous waiting periods that can only be expedited by spending more money. Most of the forms necessary for different filings can be filled out digitally and submitted online, or they can be downloaded, printed and then faxed to the designated recipient.

If you are based in a location where special business development incentives are available, be sure to check them out. Has your area suffered from a natural disaster, so that funds are now available to recover and start new businesses? Do your local or higher levels of government, or your industry sector, award grants or subsidies to encourage companies to open new markets, employ certain kinds of workers, or develop products or services in line with governmental planning goals?

With all these sources of money, be careful to not get ahead of yourself. If your regional government offers to pay for companies to attend trade fairs in new markets, for example, don't travel first and apply for reimbursement later. You will often find these aids need to be applied for and approved before the action they encourage gets started. Still, they are a great boon for start-ups and expanding businesses.

Getting Money from the Government

It's in a government's best interest to foster successful businesses. Don't be shy about checking into the resources available from all levels of government in your search for funding.

GOVERNMENTS AROUND THE WORLD are finding ways to offer assistance to start-ups and businesses that need to grow. Depending on what type of business you're in, you may be pleasantly surprised by the number of resources that are available to you. Of course, governmental programs vary from place to place, so make sure to research which options exist for you and then decide which are the most appropriate for your business.

For example if you live in the United States, the Small Business Administration (SBA) offers an array of loan programs to suit your organization's needs. Besides typical start-up loans, the SBA offers additional loan programs such as 7(a) Loans, Microloans, CDC/504 Loans and Disaster Loans. These loans can come with special mandates and restrictions regulating how they are to be used by your business. Let's look at these as representative types of loans that you may find elsewhere in the world under different names.

Start-up loans

The programs that are called **7(a) Loans** in the U.S. are special types of loans that provide financial assistance to business that have unique circumstances. Some of these may include loans for businesses that are located in rural areas, engage in exporting to other countries, and for many other special circumstances.

Microloan programs are often in the news because especially in developing countries, a very small investment can launch a stable, profitable small business, and the loan repayment rate is remarkably high. For instance, a U.S. $300 loan can allow a woman in a remote village in India to buy and run a satellite-fed smart phone. Village residents can pay her cash for the calls or Internet access they make, for example to learn what the current price is for the vegetables they grow.

Effectively, this puts the village on the phone grid without any physical lines, and everybody benefits from the entrepreneur's venture.

Microloans offered by the SBA in the U.S. can similarly deliver small, short-term loans to small businesses and to specific types of nonprofit child-care facilities. These funds are also available to selected intermediary lenders that are not-for-profit organizations with experience in lending funds as well as providing management and technical support. These agents generate loans to qualifying borrowers. The current maximum loan amount is U.S. $50,000; however most microloans are about $13,000.

Here is how you can use the capital from a Microloan:

- Use it as operating capital (for your daily business expenses)
- Buy supplies
- Buy inventory
- Buy fixtures and office furniture
- Buy equipment
- Buy machinery

Note that a U.S. business is generally not able to use the funds obtained from a Microloan to buy real estate or to service existing debts.

The SBA also runs **CDC/504 Loans**. These loans are offered through Certified Development Companies (hence CDC) and through SBA's community-based partners. This loan program is available to businesses engaging in economic development. It offers small businesses another avenue for business financing, while promoting business growth and job creation. The 504 loan program offers approved small businesses fixed-rate, long-term financing that can be used to acquire fixed assets for growth or modernization.

Disaster Loans are also available from the SBA, the Federal Emergency Management Agency **(FEMA),** the Farm Services Agency (FSA) and state governments. These loans carry low interest rates. They are available to renters, homeowners, businesses and nonprofit organizations to replace or fix personal property, machinery and equipment, real estate, inventory and assets of the business in the event of a government-declared disaster.

Grants can be a great resource for undercapitalized businesses. They are awarded to organizations that qualify under specific criteria. The great thing about grants is that they generally do not need to be paid back. Rather, they are capital contribution incentives that are dedicated to be used by businesses to invest in any number of things, with the most common being to develop products, perform research, work with emerging markets, etc.

The Risks and Rewards of Borrowing from Family and Friends

As long as you're careful, getting friends and family involved in financing your business can be a rewarding experience for everyone.

"BE ATTENTIVE AND GUARDED." This advice is like a Golden Rule for working with family or friends if you use their money to start up, run or expand your business.

Asking family and friends for money for any purpose can be a sensitive issue for most people. When the money is not for an emergency situation but rather, for your business, it can trigger a wide range of outcomes. It could lead to a feel-good moment for a family member who agrees to help you in a time of need. Or, sadly, it could create feelings of animosity and controversy. Needless to say, a lot rides on the way you handle things. So, before approaching family or friends for financial assistance, weigh the possible outcomes by considering these pros and cons.

The advantages of turning to family and friends

You may have involved family and friends as you have thought through starting a business, or as you've been growing it since then. Or, due to any number of circumstances, they are mostly in the dark about what you are contemplating. Take this into account before you open a conversation about borrowing from them. The good news is that you probably know them very, very well, and you'll know how to tune your message. But there are other advantages:

A lender with compassion: A family member or a friend may better understand your complete situation, over and above the numbers and information visible on your business plan. They probably feel a sense of pride in your willingness to pursue your dreams, and they are rooting for you to succeed. Unlike a traditional lending source, family and friends know your character, work ethic and commitment to success—things which rarely show up on a loan application.

No bank loan terms and paperwork mean savings: Family and friends might be willing to extend you more favorable terms for the loan than the bank would offer. This could stretch out your repayment schedule, reduce monthly payments, and eliminate other fees that a bank might assess. A formal application process, credit reports, documentation, etc. could also be waived, further cutting your costs. All of this can save you considerable time and money in the hunt for funding. That can be especially important if, for example, you discover a fantastic (but solid!) business opportunity on which you must move fast. Banks are generally not known for their speedy decision-making processes.

Interest rates and other factors: A family member may offer a lower interest rate than a traditional lender, representing long-term savings for you. Additionally, they may not require as much collateral (or any, for that matter) as a stipulation for lending you the money for your new business. A bank is almost certain to require this.

Flexibility re a loan or an investment: Consider, instead of borrowing from your friends or family, giving them the option of becoming investors in your business, if it works with your business model. (See the discussion of debt and equity financing on pages 73-74). This gives your prospect an alternative to just handing over the money. It also gives your prospect a form of ownership security vs. just interest on the money lent. Plus, it is possible that your prospect may have knowledge, skill, network contacts or an extensive background in your new business. These assets, in an investor in your business, could provide a different kind of helping hand in launching your business to its full potential.

The potential downside to family and friends' involvement

Most negatives related to borrowing from those near you are not so severely bad that you can't work with them. Again, your familiarity (no pun intended) with these potential backers can help you be much more sensitive to their needs, something you will probably miss if you deal with funders you're meeting for the first time, hat in hand. Still, there can be some typical scratchy spots.

Family and friends turn into supervisory personnel: Wouldn't it be great to borrow a huge sum of money from someone very close to you and then have them never bring up the subject again? The only way this may happen is if *everything* goes *exactly* according to your plan. So, it's important ensure constant reporting and follow-up on both sides of the table to keep communication clear and flowing. This will work until you report something doesn't go as planned…and that will be almost guaranteed to happen. At that point, your backers might not be as understanding as they were during the initial talks. Their concerns may prompt unwelcome meddling in your daily business (or make them feel like they have decision-making powers), which could lead to other issues beyond just the loan component. At a much lower level of drama, your backers may feel that their funding entitles them to drop by, chat, ask you to hire someone they favor or give advice during your business day, which requires diplomatic responses on your part!

Relationships can be tested: Business problems can put a strain on your relationships. Your family and friends might wholeheartedly support your business endeavor (personally and financially). However, they might not truly understand the inner workings, risks or outside factors that your new business has to deal with each day. And if business takes a turn for the worse, whether it's your fault or not, they may hold you completely responsible for any resulting damage. The same applies to your possible inability to pay off the loan they give you as well.

Stress increases: Stress is a fact of life; and owning your own business adds another layer of stress to the ordinary ones. The last thing you need is the addition of family strife! If you borrow from a bank, it takes a big risk. Even if you collateralize the loan, the bank can lose money if you default. On the other hand, when that loan is taken from family or friends, and you default, it can cost them much more than just the principle and interest they were expecting back: a sure recipe for fear, tension, anger and so forth. Lost savings, foreclosure or even bankruptcy could be in store for your backers if they were counting on you for on-time and consistent payments to them. Further, their own situation could drastically change due to illness, unemployment, and other unforeseeable events that could cause them to need their money back, and you might not be able to get replacement funding for some time. All this could be disastrous for everybody, if things don't go as planned.

Things to do if you approach family and friends for funding

The advice here is simple: Think about this approach to funding and discuss it with others first. Then, investigate the potential pros and cons from every angle to ensure your decision is based on research and facts, not emotion.

If you do decide to reach out to family and friends for funding for your new business, it is vital to prepare and conduct the exploration and execution of this transaction properly, in order to maintain balance and harmony at all times. Use the checklist provided below.

- Be professional and well prepared with your loan request presentation, just like you would for a bank application meeting (in fact, practice on Mom and Dad if you decide to go the bank route!)

- Communicate effectively, honestly and openly with all parties affected

- Give them all copies of necessary documentation so they can review them later

- Put everything in writing… everything
- Present options for lending *or* investing, if applicable
- Discuss benefits and expected outcomes of the project
- Discuss potential pitfalls and risks involved
- Lay out a comprehensive communication and reporting schedule
- If your backers decide to provide funding, draw up an agreement with an attorney's help

Statistics show that borrowing from family and friends is second only to using your own money to get a small business off the ground. During tough economic times and when banks are tightening up their lending criteria, this option will continue to be a significant way of powering up new businesses. Given great care in all stages of discussion and execution, it can be a rewarding experience for everyone involved.

Equity vs. Debt Financing

There isn't a right or wrong way to finance a business, but there definitely are methods that are better or worse for it, depending on your business's stage of development.

WHEN ACQUIRING FINANCING for your business, you will no doubt come across two of the most common forms of financing: *equity* and *debt* financing. These two basic varieties represent the majority of all financing programs used by individuals and businesses alike.

Debt financing consists of a loan (or series of loans) that must be repaid over time, almost always with interest. If qualified, a small business can borrow money with either short-term (less than one year) or long-term (more than one year) arrangements. Banks, finance companies and even some government agencies around the world are the main suppliers of debt financing. In many places there's a tax advantage attached to debt financing, since the interest you pay on your loan can be tax deductible. Debt financing has another advantage, in that your lender is not obtaining an ownership stake in your business and neither you nor they are obliged to work together further than the current loan's term, unless both parties want to make a new loan agreement.

However, debt financing also has its disadvantages. The downside to this option is that a small business may at times struggle to make timely loan payments, due to cash flow problems. This must be taken into consideration when selecting this option.

Equity financing is not a loan, but rather a capital infusion obtained from interested investors in exchange for an ownership stake in the small business. This type of financing is provided by angel investors, venture capitalists or private equity firms. Because this option is not a loan, the business does not have to repay the money invested, which can give entrepreneurs peace of mind and free them to focus on growth issues. The burden of stress shifts to delivering on the growth promised, since the investors' financial goal is to reclaim their capital infusion out of future profits.

The disadvantages of equity financing lie in degree of involvement and percentage of ownership that the investors take in your business. If you surrender more than 50% of your share, you no longer control key votes or strategies. And if your investors are inclined to engage in day-to-day involvement in your company (regardless of their ownership stake), you can end up with exhausting investor relations exercises.

Now that you know how debt and equity financing work, you need to determine which option would work best for your business. If you feel unsure in your judgment, talk with your accounting person, your tax person, and others whose experience you trust. Apart from a lot of work, there's nothing wrong in applying for both types of funding at the same time to get to a point where you can make real comparisons and come to a choice. But at least in your business's early stages, your best choice probably will be evident.

Establishing a Line of Credit

When talking about lines of credit for your business, it's best to start early in order to build up to what you could need later. The secret is to build up over time.

SMALL AND LARGE businesses alike tend to run in cycles. Cyclical ups and downs can be a result of the nature of the business's goods or services—think of New Years' decorations. Fluctuations in the economy and consumer buying patterns sometimes are cyclical too. These elements can cause a business to scramble at times to stay afloat financially. Other factors may be more or less constant in a given business. A few that keep business owners up at night are payroll requirements, too many unpaid receivables, and the need for additional inventory or equipment. As a result of all of these factors, business owners commonly encounter difficulties in effectively managing their cash flow.

Start-ups and young businesses can be particularly vulnerable to these powerful forces. Cash may be scarce for them, some or all of the time. One solution to help minimize this threat is establishing a business line of credit.

Lines of credit explained

Not just for rainy days or times of trouble, a small business's line of credit loan can actually help a small business grow and thrive. Designed to finance short-term working capital needs, i.e., to pay current bills when you know the cash you need to do so is coming in soon, a small business line of credit is administered by banks and other financial institutions to qualified businesses meeting certain minimum lending requirements.

There are two sorts of credit lines. Banks will usually extend a *secured* line of credit to most start-up ventures. This means that a personal guarantee and/or collateral of some sort will be required to gain approval of the credit line and its maximum amount. On the other hand, the lender may extend an *unsecured* line if your small business can demonstrate the credit line will involve minimum risk for the bank, through a record of consistent earnings and a positive cash flow over time.

Based on your business's credit worthiness, just like with a personal credit card, small businesses are approved for a credit line with a pre-determined maximum withdrawal amount. Once established, your business can use a revolving borrowing-and-repayment process during the term of the loan. That's why this type of financing is also known as a revolving line of credit.

Understanding the terms of the line

As a business owner you have to consider several factors before signing up for a line of credit.

- Term. Many lines of credit are for a term of one year; however, there are exceptions to this rule.

- Interest rates.

- Repayment requirements.

- Annual fees.

- Documentation needed to get the line established.

After your line has been established, it is always advisable to maintain an open flow of communication with your banker. This step affords you the opportunity to learn about transitioning out of secured to unsecured lines. Your communication also keeps you informed about the bank's other lending products that may be available to you as a result of your payment history with your current line of credit.

And speaking of payment history, there is a plus in all of this, in addition to having access to cash when you need it. A solid history of timely payments made over a period of time also improves your credit worthiness and borrowing power with the lending institution. This is an important asset, because when the time does come when your business needs more substantial financing than a credit line offers, such as a full-scale business loan or second round of financing to allow your business to expand, you'll be a more attractive candidate for that loan too. The same is true with corporate credit cards and the accompanying payment history that goes with them.

Of course, you take on a large responsibility whenever you use *OPM*— other people's money. What if you are slow or inconsistent in your repayment of the line of credit? Well, your lender may then require you to pay down your line, that is, reduce the amount you owe so the lender's risk is similarly reduced. The rule of thumb is that when you have not followed the agreed-upon payment schedule, even though the total sum borrowed may not be due for several more months, you may be asked to ramp up payments or even pay it all off as a result of violating the terms of your loan.

The path of least resistance

Many small business owners, especially in the early stages of their business's life, feel leveraged and collateralized to death. This becomes a normal feeling for more experienced entrepreneurs. The key is transitioning out of this stage by patiently building up your business's track record and then letting it speak for itself. And always remember: bankers don't like surprises. Apply for any sort of financing as far as possible before you need the funds!

Even before you start seriously thinking about seeking a line of credit for your business for the first time, there are several things you can do to help make the application process (or any application process for that matter) lead to success. One way to accomplish this is to build credit early on. Even if it may not affect your credit report or score, establishing accounts or relationships with outside entities in your business's name is vital.

- Put everyday financial services such as business banking accounts, a safe deposit box, debit cards and even a small-balance credit in your company's legal name.

- Other components could be mobile phones, subscriptions and monthly data plans, utilities and insurance coverage.

- Create an invoicing system for receivables.

- Finally, develop a history of open incoming receipts from vendors.

All these things simply add credibility to your application. They provide excellent supporting documentation when you decide to apply for a credit line.

Your goal here is to start and develop an expanding chronological file of your business dealings: externally (with vendors, etc.) and internally (with your banker and other lenders). With each transaction, and subsequently with each passing month of successful payments, your credit worthiness with the bank will take shape and expand with sustaining credentials. This clean, well-documented file will pave the way for success with other banking and financing initiatives you may be planning. Your line of credit may become a cornerstone for those plans.

In short, although a revolving line of credit can seem a major step in solving cash flow issues that may be either present or looming in a young business, you should view this stage as establishing and strengthening a bond with your banker and lending institution. A credit line is important and plays a crucial role in the early days, but it also leads positively to other support if you manage it well. Your line may stay in place indefinitely. The way in which you manage it, however, will have a major impact on your future dealings with lenders.

Using Collateral to Your Advantage

Understand this concept will help you use it wisely and
avoid getting stuck with an undesirable deal.

WE'VE ALL BEEN THERE BEFORE. All of us have needed support to work through a financial issue. Earlier, it was our parents who were first in line for our requests for advice, a bail-out, or comfort and encouragement. But after a certain point in our lives, it becomes time to seek financial assistance elsewhere. Enter: the local bank.

Today, the bank is still, for the most part, able to offer us two types of credit or loan options. These enduring options are known as secured and unsecured financing. Let's examine both.

Unsecured and secured financing

Let's start by defining an *unsecured* loan or credit extension first. An unsecured loan is a loan obtained without the use of collateral—some real thing, like a house or bank account balance that can be seized by the creditor in the event that the borrower fails to pay back properly. An individual acquiring an unsecured loan simply agrees to pay back the loan within a certain period of time, or term, based on her credit worthiness, employment history, and other factors. She will sign documents confirming these claims as part of the application process. This type of transaction is also known as a signature loan. Most credit card accounts are opened under this scenario.

But then what is a *secured* loan? It's a loan in which you pledge an asset you own that the lender would be permitted to take ownership of, in the event that you default on repayment. This allows you to obtain financing that you need but can reasonably be expected to repay, while the lender is assured his risk is minimized. Secured loans are therefore also called collateral loans.

So how does a secured loan really work? Say you need to borrow a sum of money to buy the materials you need to produce 1,000 gadgets for a new customer. You can offer your bank your delivery truck as collateral (usually the collateral is higher in value than the loan's value) and promise the bank it can sell your truck to repay your loan in case you can't make the agreed payments on time. Both you and the bank know that the truck is essential to your ability to do business, so it's a good prod to repay your loan correctly—which makes your banker sleep better at night.

Collateral therefore has enormous importance in your business's survival and success. Let's look further into how you can use collateral to secure a loan for your small business.

How a collateral loan works

As we saw above, in a collateral loan, your loan paperwork describes an asset which you promise to relinquish to the lender if you are unable to repay the loan as agreed. With that promised, the lender faces less risk and your loan request gets easier to approve. There are obviously pros and cons to this approach. Let's look at both.

Pros: Collateral of any kind secures a loan, meaning the lender can be absolutely certain that the money lent will come back—either through your repayments or through seizing and selling your collateral to repay the loan in the event you default. The stronger and more stable your collateral (which the lender will interpret to mean that it holds value that can easily be tapped), the better your chances of getting the loan approved. For example, the truck in the scenario above is easier to sell off than a truckload of tomatoes that are going bad or 100,000 pairs of shoelaces in weird colors. Additionally, strong collateral usually dictates better terms and interest rates. Usually, a well-collateralized loan can be walked through the loan process fairly quickly and with less red tape as well.

Cons: Remember, when entering into a collateral loan, you are essentially authorizing the bank to take your pledged asset from you if you are unable to repay it. Ask yourself, "Can my business afford to do without X, if for any reason we can't repay the loan?"

Also, be aware that if you are attempting to use your small business's own assets as collateral, even if it was incorporated to limit your personal liability, this particular safeguard may not totally shield you from financial exposure. Especially for start-ups and smaller businesses, a *personal* guarantee of *personal* assets still may be additionally required by the lender as a stipulation to the loan application process. So here we are back to that collateral thing again.

Types of collateral

Collateral pieces are divided into two separate categories: a) assets that you own 100 percent, outright, and b) assets that you owe on (or still carry a balance against). If you still carry a balance on the proposed collateral (such as equipment or a mortgage for a home or property) the credit grantor will examine the amount of equity (or value) the collateral encompasses to make an educated decision on how much weight the asset actually holds against the loan in question. This investigation will roughly determine the amount the bank will be able to recover if the loan goes into default mode. Here are the major forms of collateral an individual or small business might use in the secured loan process:

- Real estate (homes, land, buildings)

- Business inventory

- Accounts receivable

- Cash savings

- Deposit accounts (certificates of deposit, investment products)

- Equipment and machinery

- Vehicles (cars, trucks, tractors, boats, recreational vehicles)

- Appraised valuables (jewelry, paintings, collectibles)

But wait a minute!

You may be suddenly struck with the thought, "Hey, if I have all these assets, even cash in my piggy bank, why am I pledging them to the bank?" That's the kind of math only you can do. If you feel very confident that you can repay your secured loan and *not* put your collateral at risk, it's working for you. If you are uncertain or there are recognizable risks in the picture, think long and hard about whether you can pledge adequate collateral to get the money you need and make the payments responsibly. It's not always rosy in business, neither for you nor the bank, so be prepared to do a lot of creative problem solving every time you need to apply for a loan or credit.

Almost every individual or small business will have to investigate the possibility of a secured loan for their specific needs at some point. However, the expert business advice is quite simple here: Be organized, educated and prepared for the process. Knowing your options and uncovering the pros and cons of each option will assist you in making the right decisions regarding what to offer as collateral, how much collateral is adequate, how much risk is involved, and if a collateralized loan is the best solution for you at a given time.

What's the Lender Looking for?

Your introduction to the Three Cs of Credit.
Measure up well with them and you'll be
on your way to successful funding.

APPLYING FOR AND GETTING your first small business loan can be an exciting event. It can also be a nightmare if you're not prepared for the loan process. Much like qualifying for a home loan, to qualify for a commercial or small business loan or for a line of credit, you'll have to go through a six-step process. The steps required are usually the same, regardless of the type of loan (or the amount) you may be seeking. They include these critical phases:

- Loan application
- Pre-approval
- Processing
- Underwriting
- Approval (hopefully!)
- Closing

You must clear each hurdle of the process in order to take a seat at the closing table. But what exactly do lenders look for, anyway? In previous sections we've described the particular documents they may be seeking. And as we noted, it is important to be able to produce all documents in a timely, professional manner. These documents must be up to date and accurate in every way to support your case for receiving the financing you seek.

The Three Cs of credit

The best way to illustrate the overall prerequisites the lender may set forth is to explain the three credit measuring sticks that can make or break a loan request. They are known as the Three Cs. Let's take a look at them.

- **Character:** You are popular, successful and a pillar in the community. Everybody thinks you are highly trustworthy and your spouse thinks you're simply the greatest. That's wonderful; however, this isn't the variety of character rating that creditors are seeking. The character the lender thinks about is how you as a potential borrower have handled your past debt obligations. In essence, the lender wonders, "Are you likely to pay back the money if we lend it to you?" Lenders often look for another "C" within this category as well. It's **Consistency**. They wonder, "What does your job history look like?" or "How long have you lived in the area?" Longevity in employment and residency indicate stability. Lenders will also seek out your private credit history and personal background.

- **Capacity:** One quick way to define capacity is your present and future ability to meet financial obligations. Another way to look at it might be your income and other resources minus other debt payments. Either way, the lender wants to assess your overall capability of paying back the loan or extension of credit being considered. One crucial element of this category is the debt-to-income ratio (or DTI). Some lenders also simply refer to it as a debt ratio. This ratio is calculated by totaling your consumer debt (credit cards and installment loans) and adding to that number your housing debt (mortgage payment, property taxes and insurances). This number is then divided by your income. It looks like this:

$$[\, (\text{Consumer Debt}) + (\text{Housing Debt}) \,] \, / \, \text{Income}$$

- The acceptable debt-to-income ratio is many times dependent upon the other two Cs of Credit; and many lenders look for different ratios for different loan programs. The interest rates can also be greatly affected by your overall capacity.

- **Collateral:** As we have seen, the credit grantor may seek to use property, financial assets, or other valuables that could be employed as security to guarantee the repayment of a loan. Nearly every lender wants to be sure that you have something of value that could be sold and/or leveraged in case you default on the agreed-upon terms. A house, land, a savings or money market account, or anything with a legitimate appraised value, for example, could be used to collateralize a loan or extension of credit. Just be aware that collateral can be seized and sold if you default!

Down the road

At some point, your small business may grow and expand to the level where your personal information, collateral and/or credit rating may not be needed by the bank or other lending organizations. Your small business may decide to transition to a certain type of corporation or entity, add investors, institute a board of directors, add locations, or carry out numerous other long-range plans that will change the scope and future of your business dealings. In that case, transactions at your bank may also take on different variations as well.

However, if your business follows the same guidelines as you did as an individual when you first sought financing, the transition should be seamless. Keeping excellent records, maintaining up-to-date files, and being able to provide all the documentation the lender requests will continue to be mandatory for loan approval. But because your business now has a track record of success, it will be able to stand on its own merit in most cases.

Once your business establishes this track record, creditors and other entities will be able to access those records through outside organizations to assist them in making sound decisions on your small business. One such company is Dun & Bradstreet (http://www.dnb.com/). Often referred to as D&B, this public company, based in the United States, licenses all types of information on businesses and corporations for assistance in making credit decisions. These reports are also used in business-to-business marketing and supply chain management decisions as well. D&B maintains information on over 200 million companies worldwide. Others include Equifax, Experian, UK Credit Info and Duport.

The golden rule in practical terms

The task is easy to describe: You (and ultimately your small business) must be determined, regardless of the size, scope or nature of your business, to establish, maintain and archive impeccable records and documentation. This practice should never waver for any reason. Whether you'll be seeking to grow, gain financing, or even to sell your business, your records and documentation are what lenders, creditors and potential buyers will be examining in making their decisions.

How to Behave When Applying for a Loan

This personal aspect of entrepreneurship is important for the success of your business.

THE PROCESS OF APPLYING for a loan is more serious and complex than simply completing a loan application and submitting it to your local bank. Too many potential borrowers, and especially new business founders, fail to properly prepare their records and information before pursuing a bank loan. If you are not able to answer some key questions your banker puts to you, you can make a very poor impression, one that will be hard to reverse.

This news might seem a bit scary, particularly if you are feeling stressed because you *really need* the loan. It's time to take a deep breath, shrug off the pressure, and set yourself up to produce a really successful dog and pony act. By calling it that, we don't mean to make fun of the process or the seriousness of both your and your banker's needs to make good financial choices and decisions. We mean your image needs to be professional, polished and confident. That comes from knowing your business well and learning to think like your banker so you can deliver precisely what she needs—hopefully to approve your loan. Let's walk through the process.

Preparation

Applying for a loan obviously begins with your preparations. You need to organize certain key information for the loan application and interview. Your lender will be evaluating all the information you prepare. She's going to try to determine a number of things:

- The amount you want to borrow and how long you estimate you'll need the funds

- The risk of the loan—what chance you have of defaulting or paying late

- Your justification for the loan; what you plan to do with the money if it's approved

- Your business's ability to pay back the loan

- The collateral your lender feels is needed to secure the loan, given all the factors above

- Your individual credit strength (i.e., your private finances) as a guarantor and manager of the loan

You must consider these elements when preparing your business's financial records, business plan documents, spreadsheet forecasts for revenue and expenses, plus your personal financial statement and other relevant information. The information you prepare in your support kit must be accurate, straightforward, thorough, easy to read, and professionally laid out.

Do your best, but don't feel you have to do this solo. Your accountant, or a trusted friend who's got more experience (and a good track record!) at borrowing funds, can be very valuable as a reviewer and sounding board for polishing up your kit.

Particularly if your business is rather "young," you might want to apply to more than one lender (and here, your accountant or a friend might be helpful in making an introduction or supplying you with useful information about various lenders). In our experience, you can get a surprising array of interest rates, payment terms and other details from two or three lenders even if they are given the very same kit.

Once you have prepared all the necessary information to support your loan application, you will be set to complete the loan application document preferred by the lender(s) where you will be applying. Sometimes a question on the application can show you that you need to include, or re-position, information in your support kit.

After completing this second package of information, prepare a cover letter for the lender. Think of this letter as the written form of the verbal presentation you will give to the lender. The writing itself gives you an opportunity to organize your thoughts and compelling points about why the lender should approve your application. It will help you focus and polish your message and important key points so that when you speak with the lender, you will be very well prepared to answer all questions. As you see, preparation is key to the loan application process.

Getting set for show time

Now that you have completed a well-organized set of documents and written a well-thought-out cover letter, you can prepare for your actual loan interview. The lender may meet with you to receive all the documentation and discuss the loan request, or simply ask you to send the documents in advance of an interview. Regardless of the sequence of events, preparing for the loan interview is an important piece of the process.

Creating a good impression starts with your appearance. The first impression the lender forms of you may come from the face-to-face meeting or a telephone discussion that she conducts as a loan interview. Since most loan interviews are in person, give careful attention to your dress and appearance. Formal business attire is not always necessary, but when it doubt, dress up rather than down. In many situations, "smart casual" can work, but if you are unsure and it's possible, drop by the lender's office and take a look at what the bankers are wearing, and then match that style (or go a step more formal). The key is to dress in a manner to match the business image you wish to present to the lender. When in doubt, choose for tasteful, conservative, unobjectionable fashion in impeccable condition.

This is all about strategy. You need to consciously think about how you will behave during the loan interview. Your body language, manners, and etiquette all impact the impression you make with the lender. Small things add up to a meaningful impact, so here are some commonplace but time-honored tips for opening the conversation and then handling the presentation for best impact. As you begin the meeting,

- Maintain good posture when standing or sitting.

- Offer a friendly and sincere greeting when you meet.

- Extend your hand for a handshake if it is the appropriate custom in your area. Some cultures may prefer bowing or other gestures. (As a general tip, if you are new to the local culture, make sure you know the key do's and don'ts that apply.)

- Maintain eye contact and keep a friendly facial expression.

- Smile if the culture views a friendly smile positively.

- Expect to spend a short time establishing a connection with your contact. You might comment on some unusual feature of the lender's office, a neutral topic like the weather, or (if you know the person already) some reference to a past conversation.

- Be a focused, proactive listener. Often the art of listening well is the key to a successful conversation. You provide better responses if you excel in listening. This may be harder to do if you feel nervous, but try to silence your inner chatter anyway.

Here are some strategies to use once the preliminaries are over.

- Above all, try to anticipate and focus on your lender's interests and concerns. You could even make the transition from greeting to meeting by saying something like, "As I prepared for our meeting today I asked myself what you might want to know. So I thought I'd first tell you briefly about my business, then zoom in on our specific needs that brought me to see you today, and finally, explain how we expect to use the money you lend us. Does that work for you?"

- Always think before you respond to a question. Organize your thoughts and provide a clear, direct answer. This demonstrates your knowledge of the information and your business, but it also shows you think carefully.

- If a question is unclear to you, do not try to answer without clarification. You may come across as unqualified, stupid, or unprofessional if you respond incorrectly simply because you did not understand the question. There is no harm in respectfully asking for clarification.

- Avoid saying "I don't know." If a question comes up that you cannot answer right now, simply explain you will get back to the lender with a more qualified or more accurate response as a follow up. Note it down on the spot and don't fail to deliver.

- Be confident and self-assured but not cocky when discussing your business. You want the lender to believe in your ability to execute your plan and repay the loan.

- Avoid phrases like "I hope to achieve" or "I want to try to accomplish," and instead say "We will achieve," or "When we accomplish." Positive statements work much better than hopeful or wishful phrases. And even if you are a one-person business, use "we" in place of "I" when you mean your business. For example, say "When we receive an order, we…." Use "I" when you mean your function in the business or you're talking about something you yourself do. "When we receive an order, I first check the customer's open balance…."

- Be respectful of the lender's time and recognize when she indicates she has received all the information she needs at this time. At that moment, ask if there is any other information the lender needs. When the lender confirms she does not, then thank her for meeting with you, while rising to shake hands (or bow or whatever else, if appropriate), and preparing to exit.

- Before parting, offer to be available to the lender for any follow-up questions and reconfirm next steps and timelines politely.

- When you return to your office, send a brief cordial email (or a written note sent by mail), expressing your appreciation for the meeting and providing your contact information for any follow-up questions.

Make sure you fulfill any obligations to provide additional material or data, or whatever else you agreed to deliver, promptly and professionally. If you follow these strategies, you'll put your business in the best possible position for getting your loan approved!

CHAPTER III

Growing Your Business

Maximizing Your Cash Flow

*Money in, money out—don't let it
make you lose sleep!*

CASH FLOW MANAGEMENT is a critical key to survival and success, particularly with a new business. The nature of each business is unique, but every business aims to maximize revenue and minimize expenses. It's an ongoing process.

Payment terms

Some businesses require prepayment; others ask for payment on delivery; still others give customers payment terms that may not generate revenue for weeks, or even months. If your products must be created and held in inventory until they are sold, the total time span from incurring manufacturing expenses until revenue is received could be many months. If you provide a service, you may need to invest in training, marketing, staff and a host of other things before you deliver your first round of service, bill it and get paid, so you face the same problem as a manufacturer.

If these scenarios apply to your business, you need to manage that lag from the time you pay for your initial expenses until you receive your revenue. And this cycle repeats itself for every product or service you create, just on different schedules. Obviously, these cycles can consume significant capital, both at start-up and also for any business with growing sales. As an entrepreneur, you have to ensure you have enough capital reserves (i.e., money) or credit instruments (i.e., credit lines or loans) to cover operating expenses until your ships start coming in.

The other reality is that as your company grows, the demands for money generally get bigger. Sadly, it is entirely possible that your extended customer payment terms (receivables) combined with shorter terms you are given by your vendors for your manufacturing expenses (payables) may leave you with no money to fund the growth of sales. And that situation, when the amount of capital "in suspense" at any one time is not accessible through credit instruments or capital reserves, can lead to disasters.

Two completely different models

This may seem a little dire, but the point is to understand the importance of receiving your revenue as quickly as possible and getting the best possible terms you can for paying expenses. Ideally, you'd get paid before you put out any money or deliver anything. And there are businesses that do that: Welcome to the real world of various insurance products. The insurance industry has always been the premier example of a business sector that collects revenue in advance, while promising to pay for an insurable event in the future. By gaining the use of capital for an extended period before paying on most claims, the basic insurance model profits in two ways. First, the actual expense of administration and paying claims, when deducted from the premiums collected, usually yields a profit. Second, the premiums collected can be invested and generate additional capital for the insurance company.

The extreme opposite model is the traditional lending that banks and other primary lending institutions do. Here, the lender incurs the upfront expense by providing the money to a customer, given a promise by the customer to return the money with interest later over some prescribed timeline. Obviously, the cash flow model for a lender requires significant capital resources, in order to fund lending activities up front that will produce profit in the form of interest as loans are paid back.

Enhancing cash flow

For most businesses, cash flow requirements fall somewhere in between these extreme models. The key is to follow proven best practices that optimize your business's cash position at all times. Some of these enhance the speed with which you collect revenue and others create methods for extending the period before your expenses are due. Let's look at receivables first. Here are some effective practices for maximizing your cash in hand:

- Develop and communicate clear, written customer credit policies that specify appropriate credit limits, exact terms for payment, interest penalties, and recourse for lack of payment.

- Set a very strict schedule of payments for customers you grant higher credit limits to.

- Obtain your customer's credit card authorization, which allows you to debit the card if her invoice becomes past due. This is an excellent control mechanism for protecting your cash flow, especially with a customer who does not have strong credit. Bear in mind that an unreliable customer might also have a low credit card limit (or may have exceeded it), however.

- Provide a reasonable discount for payment within 10 days if your normal terms are up to 30 days.

- Maintain frequent and direct positive communication with customers who pass their payment due date. Don't be afraid to call daily if necessary.

- Consider offering special pricing or extra discounts in exchange for accelerated payment schedules. For example, if a customer agrees to pay all invoices within five days of receipt of goods and purchase a minimum volume of your goods and services in a given period, you can provide lower pricing. If you do this, also consider applying that discount at the end of the period in which the target is met—not on a rolling basis—to ensure you don't provide the discount and then not receive the orders you expect.

- Set up a risk deposit for a poor credit risk who is unable or unwilling to work on a Cash on Delivery (COD) method of payment. This is a sum that represents the amount of an average order (or other negotiated amount), that you may keep in the event they fail to pay an invoice by the due date. This lets you treat them as a normal billing account but still protect receipt of funds for the company.

- Explore using pre-payment, partial pre-payment, or COD terms for new customers with poor or not-yet-established credit.

And here are tips and practices to help manage your payables:

- When setting up accounts with your vendors, always go for the most favorable possible timeframe for your payments due. This might require a step-by-step process with each vendor, as some vendors will allow more time if your payment history with them has been very reliable and consistent. You might start with partial pre-payment and a balance due in stages or on some single date for your first order. Then you might progress to payment on delivery, and then to payment in 30 days, moving to 60 days, etc.

- One method to secure this consideration or others may be to pledge a back-up deposit or credit card that may only be used in the event you fail to pay on the extended due date. After some specified timeframe, the back-up provision may be revoked, if your payments have been timely.

- Pay attention daily to the cost of money based on prevailing interest rates. If borrowing money is cheap because of low interest rates, you may find it better to negotiate an additional discount for *early* payment terms with your vendors, even if it means using borrowed funds. You might achieve a larger discount for immediate payment and get a lower interest expense for the use of the money for the period of time you would have waited to pay. By borrowing the money you still kept your cash position unchanged.

- When using credit cards for paying business expenses, maintain a regimen of paying the balance in full when it comes due.

- Keep close track of the closing date for each of your credit cards. Make your purchases on a given card as often as you can during the first days of a new billing cycle. Why? Suppose a statement period closes on the 20th of January and your payment is due on February 15th. If you make your credit card purchases on this card as close as possible to January 21st, the start of the next billing cycle, you won't have to pay those charges until March 15th, about 53 days later. If you buy on January 19th, your balance becomes due on February 15th, giving you only 23-day terms.

- When purchases for your business require incremental payments for services done over time or work completed in stages, always negotiate for the least amount paid upfront as your deposit, with some reasonable portion held back until you are able to verify the satisfactory completion of the project.

The important thing to remember when looking for ways to optimize your cash position is to recognize that terms may often be a more financially important variable than price, both as a customer or as a business that serves customers. If your vendor gives you 90-day payment terms, you may find it is worth paying a slightly higher price to her rather than working with a lower-priced vendor who requires payment on delivery. The key is to always be aware of the cost of money, your specific cash flow requirements, and the options available to maximize your cash position.

Getting a Second Round of Funding

*The great news today is that there is an abundance
of opportunities for small businesses to grow.
Here's another one. Go for Round Two!*

YOU SUCCESSFULLY launched your business. Now, after some time, or after a key milestone has passed, it is safe to assume that your new business has experienced one of three likely outcomes:

- Your business has exceed all expectations

- Your business has achieved about what was forecast on the original business plan

- Uh-oh!

Regardless of what has transpired during the initial stages of your new business's evolution, one common denominator probably played a significant role in deciding the size, scope, scale and even the success of your undertaking: funding. As you well know, funding is a critical. It is a force that can dictate how and when a business starts, influence the future growth and expansion of that business, be a life-saving mechanism during tough economic times, or kill the business against all odds.

Many small businesses can be started using personal collateral, some financial assistance from family or friends, a small business loan from your local bank, or a combination of those funding sources. And usually, once the business has gotten out of the starting gate, that initial round of funding can be used as you see fit, too. The catch: from marketing and advertising to payroll, the monies you acquired for start-up and early survival must represent funding well spent.

Second-round funding basics

Many factors can come into play when a new business is attempting to expand or get to the next stage. It happens in larger, established companies, too. So, regardless of your company's age or market position, second-round funding may be necessary to accomplish the goals you've set for your company. It usually is secured through one or more sources. The process usually takes place after the initial start-up phase, when a business is able to successfully demonstrate that it is positioned for growth.

As an entrepreneur, where do you go for second-round funding? The obvious first stop might be your local bank. But what if your business is unable to use secure debt financing? What if you are unable to acquire sufficient financing through a traditional business loan? There are other alternatives.

Enter private equity

When it comes time for a small business to seek an additional supply of working capital for growth, it may turn to the world of private equity. Private equity investments are made, by and large, by private equity firms, venture capital firms and/or angel investors. Each of these types of investor has a unique set of objectives, partialities and investment strategies. One common theme among them, however, is delivering the necessary working capital to the applicant. That funding can be used to support growth, deliver new products and services to the market, fund research and development initiatives, enable buyouts, or even restructure a business's ownership, operations, or management structure.

Which funding source is the best for you? Well, most small businesses turn to angel investors for their second round of funding needs. Angel investors can be portrayed as affluent individuals or a grouping of proactive individuals who make financial investments (equity financing) in start-ups or in businesses that may be in their early stages of life. They are investors who usually provide their own funds, versus a pool of funds, in exchange for convertible debt or ownership equity. In many cases, this type of private equity can bridge the gap between loans from family, friends and traditional banking or lending organizations to the next level. Angel investors also are usually willing to take bigger risks and/or invest in projects that traditional lenders are unable to accommodate due to the nature of the investment itself.

Three scenarios… one objective

With countless uncertainties popping up all the time, a small business owner has to always be prepared for what lies ahead, even if he or she is unaware of what precisely the uncertainties are. These factors are usually what dictate how a business fares, especially in its early stages of existence. In many instances, a second round of funding addresses those unforeseeable factors. As we've seen, there are basically three outcomes that a business could realistically experience: smashing success, as-expected performance, and tanking. So, if and when a second round of funding is deemed necessary, knowing there are alternatives in addition to your local bank can be reassuring.

But what do angel investors (or other private equity firms) look for in an investment? The same thing a bank would look for: a healthy and positive return on their capital infusion. These investors will require some of the same criteria a bank does. Here's a sample of what they may request:

- Solid business, marketing and strategic plans for growth

- Financials

- An established ownership/management team with industry experience and proficiencies

- A breakdown of the sources of funding you used to start your business

- A comprehensive overview of your market and your current market position

- Competitive advantages that your products and services enjoy

- A return on investment outline and forecasting

- An exit strategy for the investor in a defined period of time

When is the proper time to seek second-round funding? It may sound glib, but you'll probably know it when you see it.

In addition, every investor, angel group or other private equity firm has its own qualifying factors that determine when (and how) the process will commence. The Internet is an invaluable place to begin your search queries regarding which type of organization might be best suited for your current situation and ultimately your future needs. Many organizations even allow you to apply online for pre-approval and future consideration. Some funding organizations may have minimum standards for this feature, and fees may apply as well.

The great news today is that there is an abundance of opportunities for small businesses to gain additional competitive advantages in their markets with a fresh infusion of working capital. Many of these alternatives to the traditional lender didn't exist years ago either, giving you more options. As always, being educated and in-the-know regarding what's available to you and what might be the best fit for your specific funding needs will be a major step in the right direction.

Forecasting Your Growth

*Tea leaves? Crystal balls? The real name
of the game is to be realistic.*

IF YOU HAVE ANY HOPES of having a successful first round of fund raising for your business, *don't* put together a series of monthly, quarterly, annual, three- and five-year projections showing how your new product or service will soar from zero to a huge profit within the first year. This is unlikely. Moreover, when you start representing your start-up as such you are simply going to turn off potential investors.

Most investors are skeptics for a reason. It's not because they don't believe in you or your idea. But rather, because everyone has the next big idea, everyone's idea is worth millions and everyone's idea will sail flawlessly to the top of whatever market or industry in which they operate. Unfortunately this is not usually the case. In fact, most businesses, even those that are successful and yield plenty of ROI (return on investment), are not the biggest, best, top earning, most profitable ones, nor are they those with the most market share. They are somewhere in the middle.

Now, if you legitimately have a new, never-before-seen "mouse trap" that the entire world has to have, then maybe you can get away with such a circus. But for most of us, it's more about building a strong foundation, plowing in lots of hard work and hoping just to get the business to a profitable state that is ready for growth. I can't tell you how many business plans have come across my desk with the most ridiculous forecasting and performance expectations. It only takes a second to see through it all. At that point I usually throw the plan in the trash bin, along with any of those showy, super-expensive credit card-like business cards that come with them. (I'll dig into my problem with those silly cards later.)

It's important to forecast your anticipated financials conservatively and demonstrate on paper that even with the most minimal results, your business can survive. Notice I said survive, not rack in millions. This is because you are usually the one dreaming of the "big win," while an investor is simply looking at risk.

Most individuals and businesses that may invest in your business are looking to either minimize risk or invest in projects or businesses that are risk adverse. I would recommend performing a sensitivity analysis, outlining how much you can be off of target and still achieve profitable operations. I would even go as far as mapping out a worst-case scenario model, showing how even under harsh circumstances, your business model is sound. Conversely, if you cannot generate a forecast model showing "below plan" or "below target" performance that still maintains healthy levels of operation, then you may need to reconsider the particular project or initiative.

Another important thing to remember in regard to lofty goals and projections is that such plans typically land in the trash. Not because business plans are garbage. But because the thought process that put the forecasting together is not here in reality with the rest of us. Understanding the entrepreneur's forecasting style helps me understand if they are thoughtful and logical in their approach, or if they are on a completely different planet with regard to business.

This sounds dumb, but it's serious. Some individuals are so in love with themselves and their pet project that they start to believe their own press clippings and the bluffing that comes along with their off-the-cuff planning.

And back to those hard plastic business cards that each cost a fortune. I simply take them as a demonstration of the owner's misplaced focus regarding the spending priorities of her business. It drives me nuts when small business owners and founders of start-ups looking for funding throw solid plastic business cards on my desk that cost more than a cup of designer coffee. That may not sound like much, but when you know they ordered 500 to 1,000 of them instead of having a copy center make perfectly decent ones for next to nothing, you can see they aren't business oriented. Also, it's just irritating to have yet another plastic card to shove in my wallet. It's already over flowing with more of the same.

M.O.

Just Grow It!

You may reach a point when you're fed up with planning. But it's so much better than failing. And yet...

PLANNING AND ORGANIZING all the details and elements in your budget or initiative is a complex, comprehensive process. Each idea you develop and every initiative you organize leads to more and more planning, more budgeting. The danger lies in getting caught up in perpetual *planning*, leading you to neglect getting important growth initiatives *launched*.

The key is to establish a clear timeline for any initiative. Make it your first step when you begin your planning. Your timeline must include specific deadlines for each segment of the planning process, with clearly stated deliverables due at each of those deadlines. The interim deadlines and deliverables should lead up to the final deadline for the launch of the entire initiative.

If you encounter any delays or changes in the expected deliverables, check carefully to determine if the final launch deadline can be maintained. If not, quickly identify what needs to be done to adjust other elements to meet the ultimate launch deadline. Building an effective project or initiative timeline and delivering what's needed on time is key to the success of your launch.

Setting the standard

As a founder and leader of your company, your performance can set up standards for others in your group. Your discipline, focus and tenacity in strictly following the timeline and delivering what's needed on time, regardless of the sacrifices in time and energy required, is the formula for achieving success in many aspects of your business. Focused, timely action is key to getting a good initiative launched. But more important, it will establish the standards by which your company will succeed in the future.

Plan, then act; plan, then act

It is also important to remember that great planning becomes worthless without taking effective and timely action. It's always necessary to balance planning and action. Failure to execute on either one can lead to a very poor or negative outcome. It may seem important and effective to spend an endless amount of time planning an important initiative, but failing to execute on a reasonable timeline may lead to procrastination and paralysis for the business.

Alternatively, taking action too rapidly without the guidance of effective planning can lead to costly mistakes and missed opportunities. The key is to balance both planning and action with an effective timeline you follow aggressively.

What if the wheels come off?

Sometimes it may be necessary to honestly recognize that you simply cannot meet deadlines. If delays seem to be overwhelming the process, it is important to break the chain of events and re-establish momentum with a fresh timeline and revised deadlines. At this point, taking action is critical to getting the initiative started. It may be necessary to make some decisions and move forward without 100 percent of the information gathered and 100 percent of the details completed. Avoid analysis paralysis and know when it is time to get going and execute the plan. There is a point when action is key and it is simply time to get off your chair, leave your office and *just grow it!*

Methods of Growth

*The best method depends entirely on you and your
business. It helps to know the process.
Find what's best for you.*

REGARDLESS OF how far your entrepreneurial spirit has already taken you, let's go ahead and assume you've already launched your small business successfully. In the midst of getting from the start-up phase to a smooth-running machine, there were most likely several goals or milestones that you set as a road map for reaching consistent stability.

You may have sought advice from experts and mentors. You may have also gotten educated by gaining industry experience, researching the Internet, reading trade publications or attending seminars. You probably invested sweat equity, money and other personal resources along the way too. In the end, it was all worth it as you got your small business off the ground.

So… what's next?

If you've actually survived the battles of a start-up and then subsequently built a successful business, you may wonder what next steps are fundamental in growing your business beyond its present status. There are abundant options and countless methods to get you to the next level. Let's concentrate on two things here. First, let's do a very quick review of the past to ensure you've covered a few basics; and then let's consider a few elements that can foster the growth for your small business.

A quick checklist to review

Whether you accomplished these things in getting where you are or you are still attempting to get out of the starting gates, make sure most, if not all of the basic steps below have been completed before you seriously consider trying to engage in any type of growth.

- **Create an identity**. Build a brand, create a market position, offer unique selling points, let others know how you stack up to the competition.

- **Create some relationships**. Establish a solid client base, stay in touch with repeat customers, ask for referrals, join trade associations or business groups, establish strong connections with your banker, accountant, and legal representation.

- **Create a presence in the community**. Volunteer, do charity work, join various associations, donate to worthy causes, be a positive activist for your community.

- **Create some history**. Establish a track record of solid sales and happy customers, deliver solid results to investors, keep your banker and accountants happy with month-after-month records of solid returns and up-to-date documentation on everything.

These basics form a solid cornerstone for preparing for future growth. They should never be ignored or taken for granted. The combination of all of these external efforts with your internal documentation and records (such as your business, marketing and strategic plans; official corporate and legal documentation; tax filings; banking records; etc.) establishes yours as a well-run business, one that has good odds of success in climbing to the next level or seriously expanding. If you've made it this far, it may be time to plan for growth. You will face important decisions regarding the specific methods, strategies and modes you will choose to take your business to the next level.

Methods, strategies and modes of growth

Just as it paid off for you to develop a rational, fact-based business plan to help you identify and anticipate challenges when you started your business up, it will pay off now to plan consciously how you want to grow.

Methods of funding: The way you finance your growth plan may end up being the most significant decision you make for the long-term future of your small business. As we've said, your two options are debt financing and equity financing (see pages 73-74 for more on this).

Strategies: Considering alternative growth strategies is also vital as you think about your growth process. Not all will fit your business, but it's wise to think broadly before you narrow things down and select those that are most in tune with your products and services. Here are a few strategies to start your thinking process.

- **Diversify.** Think of adding new and/or alternative products and services to the ones you already offer. This strategy can be hugely successful with a solid and long-standing client-base. It adds new income streams to the existing ones, and many times these products and services can be successfully bundled.

- **Head to the Internet, think about apps.** You no doubt already have a website. It might be a down-and-dirty start-up version or a fancy site. But either way, as you stage for growth, it's vital to perform a comprehensive review of what your site looks like, how it functions, and what it could do for you if it were revamped. Is your small business able to offer any of your products or services on an e-commerce platform? More and more buyers are heading online to make purchases, large and small. As part of your review, ensure that your branding, marketing and messaging are singing in unison to deliver a knockout punch to potential clients. Frequently, start-ups don't have smoothly consistent branding and marketing in their first stage, so here's a chance to clean up the clutter and refine your positioning. Finally, consider whether mobile applications are yet another way to expand this option outside the traditional brick-and-mortar selling platform. Can they help your growth?

- **Open a new location.** This strategy can be expensive and risky; however if financing is in place, you've done your homework thoroughly, and the signs are positive, go for it. Additional locations can add to your visibility and outreach in your market and create a more convenient way for your customers to buy from you. Just don't fool yourself if the signs are not convincing.

- **Expand to a new market.** Do your products or services already thrive in the market in which you operate? If so, could you experience equal success in a contiguous market? Again, careful, proper homework will dictate which market(s) will be best suited for this option.

- **Look into franchising, licensing and private labeling.** All of these options can be viable alternatives for expanding your company's footprint. Franchising your entire business to other markets and locations, licensing specific products and/or services to others, and private labeling your popular offerings could yield huge results. Some businesses have done all of them; some choose one particular route to take with these strategies. Not every small business is suited for these options, but try brainstorming to see if these strategies offer you a way to get other parties to move your products and services for you.

- **Offer commissions to outside sources.** If applicable (and also if legally acceptable, in certain industries), every small business should investigate paying outside sources for selling or re-selling your products and services or for referring clients to your business. As always, an ethical review should accompany this strategy to ensure proper business practices are followed. But, if everything seems to be satisfactory, having others work for you and refer on your behalf can be a boost to your bottom line.

Modes: Finally, the mode in which you grow needs consideration. There are two clear environments that your small business could select as the best alternative to expanding.

- **External growth** involves more significant financial resources in most cases, and can also require years of research and dedicated time. Mergers and takeovers are two external modes of financial growth. A **merger** is the combining of two or more companies, usually with the approval of all companies involved along with any affiliated shareholders and/or directors.

- A **takeover** (also known as an **acquisition**) is a corporate action where an acquiring company makes a bid for another company. The response by the board of directors and/or shareholders agreeing upon the terms of the agreement dictates if the takeover is *friendly* or *hostile* in nature.

- **Internal growth** involves a business escalating its size and capacity through investing in its own existing collection of products and services or by developing new ones. This process is also referred to as *organic growth*. Oftentimes, it requires long-term development; however, it is widely viewed as less risky than external growth alternatives.

It can be a refreshing, positive exercise to investigate the numerous means of growth and to explore the many growth opportunities available to you as a small business owner. You may find that you must prioritize or set schedules for attempting the most promising ones, as your funding for growth and other resources will have definite limits. But by keeping these points in mind, you should be able to identify some winning approaches to evaluate and refine further. Doing your homework will eliminate some options and elevate others to the forefront of discussion. Making timetables flexible for planning and taking these decisions will help ensure good thinking. Finally, don't be afraid to bring in other entrepreneurs, experts and even consultants to validate (or refute) your research along the way.

Growing Global

You can feel the world growing smaller every day.
Why not profit from that?

NO MATTER WHERE in the world your business is based, *growing* it is fundamental to your continued financial success. If the product or service you provide travel and adapt well, your business's growth can be sped up and achieved through a variety of sales and marketing initiatives that reach potential customers in markets worldwide.

Most conventional businesses start life supported by sales in a geographic area that surrounds their initial location. Not long ago, the cost of acquiring distant customers, the logistic expenses needed to sell to and to follow up with them, and the resource requirements to support long-distance programs limited the initial territory a business could target.

The shrinking world

But that's no longer the only scenario. Constantly evolving improvements in technology, communication tools and Internet capabilities have greatly enhanced the efficiency of pursuing global sales for many businesses, even from Day 1.

Of course, there are challenges. Significant research will be required to understand all the variables necessary to conduct business with customers in different parts of the world and with different cultural biases. This research requires an investment of time and money, but your insights may yield a broad range of market opportunities you have not already penetrated. Gathering all of this information will prepare you for global sales expansion into the markets you identify that seem like practical opportunities.

Your business may face specific requirements, regulations, tariffs, import and export duties that may impact the practical capabilities for sale of your goods or services internationally. Translation, localization (adapting for the local market's values, customs, and other factors), currency issues, legal and bookkeeping rules and laws, production, transport—plus simply trying to figure out if what you offer will satisfy customers' needs in the target market—will basically require you to build a separate business plan for your global expansion. As always, developing your business plan will flush out issues and questions you need to pay attention to, but it's worth the effort.

Thinking globally may be a new experience for your business, but there are tools, services and people with track records you can tap if you need them. Technology, especially communications technology, is moving at an accelerating pace. We are able to communicate globally via email, cellular phone, videoconference, and instant messaging tools that continue to shrink the distance between all parts of the world. While working face-to-face with customers and associates has great advantages, it's no longer always necessary to travel, given these powerful connections.

It may be worthwhile to work with specialists to conduct your market research and later execute global sales and marketing initiatives abroad. Governments offer often surprising levels of support, usually in key cities abroad, to assist their citizens in making contact with and finding resources to support international growth. Some also provide investment credits, subsidize travel and trade show attendance, and so forth for their nationals who are starting up in new international markets.

But what if your business cannot afford outside help and your government has limited support services? You can still do it yourself! If you can commit the necessary time, you can do the spadework mostly from home. The secret is to start small and expect to grow slowly, making mistakes and learning from them as you go along. It's wise to target the most promising market and get that up and running, then move to second-tier markets as your business adapts to the unique challenges of international business. Also, consider trying to find a local partner in your target market, a company or person with a natural fit for your offering, rather than trying to master every last detail and working long distance in an unfamiliar territory. It may prove to be a first stage in a progression of steps that end up with your company working independently, so regard that option as potentially free education.

For one thing, you probably will develop a completely different global perspective about the design and execution of your sales and marketing initiatives. Consider all possible elements available for connecting with and selling to customers in your target market. They may include social media, email marketing initiatives, website advertising programs, shared website links, telephone programs, text messaging options, webinar sales and information programs, chat rooms, blog postings, and website resources and interactive tools. But for some parts of the world, selling gadgets or advertising your service at street markets or bazaars, or door to door, or in schools may be your best choice.

The important points to remember are the research you need to do to choose the best global market opportunities, the profile of customers and their needs in each target area, the prevailing culture and language, the local business practices, and local contacts you can cultivate to help you grow. The ability to grow globally rests on your ability to think globally and reach out to the worldwide market with an open mind—and a taste for adventure!

CHAPTER IV
Avoiding the Roadblocks

The Dilemma of Stagnated Success

Even if you are barely started in business,
it's wise to see the bigger picture.

THERE ARE FIVE important stages of business to understand when monitoring the ongoing financial health of your developing business. These different stages in the life of the business are related to a number of internal and external forces. Being aware of them and working to avoid getting trapped in a given stage requires discipline and focus on the key elements of each one.

The Start-Up Stage of the business is a delicate balance between planning, organizing, aggressive sales initiatives, stringent cost controls, and dynamic adjustment to frequently changing information and results. Frankly, it can be chaotic. Entrepreneurial enthusiasm, pushing through roadblocks hundreds of times before achieving the results you need, drives the company's life. Energy, focus, persistence, constant adjustment, and unwavering determination are key elements in start-ups. Financially, things can look good, if the company has realistic cash reserves or access to credit to support it until revenue starts coming in. As a company continues to grow and gain momentum, this start-up stage shifts into the Development stage.

The Development Stage sees things perking along (provided the company survived Start-Up) and the focus shifts to achieving growth goals. There's still a lot of energy and enthusiasm, but things are starting to settle down and processes that enhance efficiency or improve quality begin to claim a share of everyone's attention. Financially, budgeting and cash flow, forecasting, credit management and improved reporting systems get a lot of attention.

The Maintenance Stage of Business appears when a younger, growing business matures into a more stable, consistent structure with established customer relationships, relatively steady business volume, and comprehensive elements to maintain and support the more mature business structure. In this cycle a large portion of the business infrastructure is focused on maintaining and supporting existing business relationships and product segments that drive the bulk of the profit for the company.

In this stage, however, a lower percentage of resources may be devoted to starting new products, programs and initiatives, while infrastructure and the status quo rise in importance. The danger in this is that the energy and momentum that was used to start and develop the initial business success may be lost or severely reduced. Without the appropriate focus on new products, new programs, innovation, and researching new trends, the company may begin to stagnate. Its products and services may become less compelling to the changing market, and competitors with fresh new ideas, products and programs may start eroding market share. At this point, stagnation may start a downward financial spiral.

The Declining Business Stage unfortunately sometimes follows, often marked by significant stagnation and incorrect actions taken to re-establish business momentum. The common mistake made in trying to reverse stagnation is a failure to assess its true causes. Not recognizing the changing needs of the market; failing to adjust, evolve or replace the product; backing off on sales and marketing initiatives; avoiding making real comparisons to successful competitors; and an inability to openly assess weaknesses all contribute to the downward spiral of a business. As we have seen around the world in recent years, a debate arises: do we choose austerity, or invest in future growth with OPM (other people's money)?

Too often, management gets caught up in spending most of their time building defensive reports and statistics to prove their past successes will enable them to turn things around and achieve positive results again. They fail to accept that the current plan is not working and change is needed. But change can only occur if management is willing to open their minds, check their egos at the door and explore all possibilities openly and honestly.

To halt the decline, a number of things need to happen. The process starts with SWOT analysis (strengths, weaknesses, opportunities, and threats) of who is successful and why. It also includes market research about what customers want today and in the future. Only then can a very candid and open review of the current business related to this new information happen. A very aggressive and focused strategic planning session follows, to develop an effective plan to effectively re-start and grow the business.

Unfortunately, all too often the leadership and management responsible for a declining company are usually not the best-equipped people to recognize this problem and execute the solution. This is why a declining company often lives with management in denial long enough to slide into the final stages of shutdown, turn around, or sale.

The Turn-Around Stage looks very much like the initial start-up stage because of the fast-paced tempo needed to get things going in the sales area while controlling costs aggressively. The Finance area needs to back this new outlook while making sure expenses and investments are still duly evaluated. The company is back on uncharted waters and its past successes don't necessarily promise future ones.

Also, unlike in the lean and mean Start-Up stage, in Turn-Around the company must deal with any number of pre-existing elements of the business that need to be addressed while simultaneously turning on new sales momentum and growth. These additional elements include aged debt, infrastructure, employees, existing customers, suppliers, vendors, and other established elements. In some cases layoffs and job eliminations are necessary. Restructuring debt may be required to allow the company to operate. Customer relationships may need to be repaired and rebuilt. Vendor relationships may need to be repaired or changed. The complexity of the turnaround environment is a blend of removing the old elements that do not fit the new model, establishing the new strategic direction in a very short period of time, and executing on all initiatives as quickly as would happen in a start-up cycle of business. A successful turnaround requires candid, open conversation with a group of dedicated team members willing to follow and execute the leaders' decisions quickly and efficiently.

The different stages of business and their financial aspects are important to understand as you start and grow a new business. Stagnation can creep in when the drivers that were responsible for your success get lost in a more complacent, stable business environment. Success is not a permanent state, however. The journey you started on Day 1 must never end. You can steer clear of stagnation if your company keeps growing, innovating, and pursuing the evolving needs and wants of your customers. The future success of your business depends on staying focused on the most successful track.

Facing Your Financial Fears

*The first step to overcoming your financial fears is to face
them. That step is always the hardest. But if you
face them, you can overcome them.*

IF YOU CASUALLY ASK people to name their fears, their responses will be all
over the map. Some may immediately point to death, personal tragedy or natural
disasters. Others might mention actual phobias such as a fear of heights, the dark
or even spiders. But whatever they might be, we know we can't avoid our fears
forever. Completely ignoring them won't make them magically disappear.

In business (as in your personal life), your approach to financial fears may
follow the same path as some of your other fears or phobias. You may ignore
them. You may have someone else deal with them; or you may simply struggle
through them with great trepidation. So, what are some common financial fears
that many entrepreneurs share? Let's look at a handful:

- Running out of money before revenue or profitability arrives
- Investing too much new money back into the business
- Losing customers or market share
- Borrowing money
- Taking out loans
- Opening bills (yes, opening envelopes or clicking on links!)
- Paying bills late
- Not having enough funds to pay the bills, payroll, taxes
- Invoicing
- Asking for payments
- Collecting late fees
- Not keeping records well, especially for tax purposes

- Not making consistent, appropriate financial decisions for the business
- Not being able to sell your company for a profit
- Justifying the sale price for the company
- Not being able to retire at a suitable age
- Having no exit strategy

Every small business owner will eventually experience one or several of these fears, or similar ones. Common sense says that facing your financial fears, developing a clear understanding of the situation, defining what's controlable and what's not, and exploring what might be at stake will set you up to deal with them much better.

But what if you haven't had much experience in these fear-generating areas? What if you've previously failed at some of these things? Regardless of the predicament, it's best to confront your most significant financial fear(s) head-on, treat them like a high priority to-do list item, and then begin reducing each of them to a manageable size.

Taking this course of action will give you a more empowered perspective from which you can begin to map your moves toward a positive outcome. As long as financial fear grips you, you'll feel paralyzed, and nothing will ever get resolved. You will find that if you start thinking and acting differently, proactively, you can build a new habit and a new response to the flags of fear. You will get better at handling them now and in the future, get even better and better. Who wants a life of overall worry and constant indecision?

Confront your fears with relevant questions

Start by turning your focus away from your fears to the real facts, and then start trying out or evaluating solutions mentally or on paper. This will begin removing some of the mystery behind the scary things. Move your probable fears out in the open before they actually occur by asking questions like the ones below. They are designed to get you thinking about that big bear growling in the corner of your mind.

- What is my back-up plan if the business begins to falter?
- How much am I willing to invest in my business?
- What will be my strategy for attracting and then maintaining a strong customer-base?
- What will be my survival strategy in a slow economy?
- How much will I be willing to personally collateralize on a business loan or line of credit?
- How much should I budget for expenses and outstanding invoices?
- What do I want or need my company to be worth when I sell it?
- At what age do I want to retire?

Take control, evaluate and plan ahead

Asking a series of precise, financially-related questions even before your business launches also will force you to look at nearly every financial scenario (and subsequent fear) that could come into play *before* it actually happens. The result could be that your fears may never materialize, or they may end up being nothing more than a few challenging roadblocks to overcome.

Throughout the course of this exercise, you may not initially have all of the solutions covered. This is not a big deal. The bigger picture here is that you have undertaken a process to eliminate your financial fears by facing them, thinking them through, and taking action. Here are some simple guidelines to follow as you begin assembling your questions and search for actionable responses:

Be realistic. Don't understate or overestimate the potential of your new business, especially the financial aspects of the operation.

Set no-nonsense financial goals. It's great to aim high. Wanting your business to achieve its maximum potential is only natural. However, thinking of the financial facets that surround your organization, these goals must be judged feasible by not only you, but your partners, investors and employees.

Document your existing financial affairs. Knowing and understanding all the ins and outs of the current financial status of your business will determine not only where you've been, but where you might be going—and where you're vulnerable. This aids in proper forecasting and proposed budgeting all the way around. Knowing exactly where you really stand, even if it's not a place you want to be, takes the guess-work out of the equation too.

Make financial literacy an ongoing part of your entrepreneurship. Knowing how credit, credit-scoring, banking, lending, investing and even accounting work is one the most significant gifts you could ever give for yourself and your business.

Involve industry professionals at every turn. When in doubt, turn to the pros. Once you have educated yourself in relevant financial areas, it will be easy to communicate your business's needs to these professionals, who should then be able to receive the hand-off from you with minimal confusion. Your financial fears should be eased even further, since you know that your team of legal, accounting, bookkeeping and banking professionals are keeping a watchful eye on the financially-related elements of your operation.

Your former fears are now an action plan

Facing financial fears is something that virtually all entrepreneurs have experienced. For you and your small business, the goal will be to turn those negative financial fears into a practice of positive financial oversight. This oversight can be done with confidence if you have a solid and affirmative plan in place to convert those pointless fears. Your new plans will now establish a current (and future) roadmap to follow to keep you on the path to financial success.

Remember, your financial fears may simply be opportunities in disguise. So, be confident, get educated, take action, and then get in control. Success awaits.

How Much Should You Share with Employees?

It's not just about profit. Information is almost as coveted as cash. Ever heard of the inner circle?

IF YOU HAVE employees in your small business (or intend to hire some in the future) you face countless decisions surrounding them. One key aspect of successfully managing employees is keeping them happy and productive. At some point you will have to make choices about the level of transparency you establish regarding sensitive company news. Sharing information with employees can build morale and productivity, but it requires good judgment and a good feel for people.

Think about your company for a moment. Do you currently tell your employees everything that is going on? Do you tell them nothing? Or do you provide information only about matters you think they need to know about?

You're the boss, right?

Obviously, certain things need to be kept confidential or be adapted before sharing. Salary rates, benefits, employee records, or other human resources-related materials need protection. Ditto for any sensitive corporate legal proceedings, private records and trade secrets. This information should always be protected, explicitly through non-disclosure agreements, hiring agreements and the like; or implicitly or verbally in the context of meetings, conversations and correspondence.

Early on, some small business owners may lean toward limited information sharing with their employees. They hope to control the work environment and keep people focused on their particular tasks. So they only give out information on a *need-to-know* basis. But sometimes this top-down control approach can backfire, as employees may assemble the limited scraps of information they hear into distorted pictures laced with speculation and gossip—which is likely to be incorrect, and is potentially more distracting and morale-lowering than carefully concealed business issues.

Other entrepreneurs err on the side of letting everyone in on every headache and triumph. When your entire company can fit in one vehicle and you share one open office, it's hard for things to be otherwise. This does tend to distract people who don't know the context of what they overhear, who lack financial or other training to understand issues, or who just love to listen in on the office dramas. It can give employees a sense of participating in the new business's success, though, and can teach people how their specific role fits with the rest of the business.

Employees, for the most part, want to feel proud of where they are employed and in the work they produce. As an entrepreneur, you must chart a course that's neither secretive nor tell-all when it comes to sharing company news. If you strike the right balance, you'll create a win-win situation for everyone. Inadequate information can cause operational and cultural dysfunction while indiscriminate sharing bogs everybody down. Balanced transparency often keeps your best staffers from leaving. If members of your team get adequate information to maximize their performance but are protected from undue worries and stress, they can work with satisfaction and feel a sense of belonging in the organization.

How do you create balanced transparency?

Let's take a look at a few things you can do if you want to open up the flow of information to help create a positive work environment.

Make transparency a resolution. Routinely providing employees news, updates and information about the company, its customers, and the current projects can go a long way in making people feel like a true member of a team and also an integral part of the company itself. Such sharing can provide stability, confidence and focus across the board. Consistently communicating this information also helps build trust throughout the group. By implementing a certain level of transparency within an organization, you can make certain that your staffers have all the essential information. And bit by bit their own business savvy will grow, making them more valuable employees over time.

Create a two-way communication and feedback model. Generally, the more constructive feedback you can offer your employees, the more they will benefit. And you can benefit from feedback as well. When employees can acknowledge their progress, or lack thereof, and clearly understand how their current priorities fit with the bigger company picture, they will become more effective. The same goes the other way too. Receiving feedback from workers regarding your new products, customer service issues, pricing, future project feasibility and even your leadership and management can be invaluable asset for an owner in reaching decisions. An environment of mutual respect and support can tap hidden talents when balanced transparency is part of the mix.

Place a high priority on company-wide collaboration. Once transparency is established and a feedback and communication model is implemented, a company-wide collaboration plan could also be part of the regular communication stream. When your workforce has a platform to candidly discuss goals and projects with owners and managers, creativity and innovative concepts will flourish. This encourages employees to be proactive in solving problems themselves too. By updating them on progress on projects they have initiated, you show their contributions are helping to grow and improve the business. Display or share charts, graphs and reports to mark progress.

Are there risks in this policy?

Of course there can be, if you're not careful. It would be a serious mistake to use this new transparency as a crisis management device. The last thing you want is to scare your employees to death about their employment status with you. If you are facing layoffs or similar negative events, it might be wise to bring in a human resources specialist to either coach you or actually handle the communications properly for you. Truth is, if you've been sharing good and bad news along the way, even very bad news can be put into context and make sense. Your employees know it's a tough world out there, and that your company (or any company for that matter) can be vulnerable to internal or external factors that could lead to trouble.

But consider the alternative. Employees may assume the worst and even jump ship when they are not communicated with by their business owner. Consistent silence can cause negative rumors, panic and even anger sometimes. None of these reactions contribute to a creative or productive work environment.

Of course, getting everyone together for the sheer purpose of sounding an alarm is never the correct course of action. Sharing tough information carefully and respectfully can show your employees that you are leading with confidence in tough times. It can inspire people to tackle roadblocks in a collaborative effort. Everyone can benefit if they forge a team environment in heading off the negatives that could be on the way. Confidence rules over crisis every day.

Finally, always temper bad news and information with the positives that surround you. A company full of solid employees who understand what's at stake and who are willing to work together to solve problems in a positive environment is always better than the alternative.

Your challenge is to figure out what level of transparency and course of action may be best suited to your organization's business model. Therefore, do not take this project lightly. Regard it as the foundation of employee contentment, longevity and success.

Common Financial Pitfalls

By avoiding these common pitfalls, you can
start out where everyone else wanted to be.
Know what you don't know.

THE SINGLE smartest thing to remember as a small business owner is to *know what you don't know!* And although that statement sounds funny when spoken, it's absolutely true. Every entrepreneur dreams of launching his or her dream company without any hitches—and financial hitches always top that list.

With that in mind, just understanding that an assortment of financial pitfalls might be on your path going forward will be half your battle. On the other hand, the future can be hard to anticipate when you are starting up. You can learn from other people's experience by asking yourself how likely their misfortunes could be to happen to you, and then asking how you would respond if they do pop up. That may not be much comfort, but by envisioning typical scenarios, you can prepare as much as possible.

Common threats and what to do about them

So what are the most common threats to a small start-up? And what can you do to minimize your business's chance of running into them? Here is a list of the most common ones, based on our experience and our familiarity with many other entrepreneurs' challenges. Then below, we'll suggest the best ways to avoid them.

Here are the threats, in no particular order of importance or frequency:

- Not having enough cash reserves to support operations until revenue from the business starts flowing in

- Using credit cards to finance operations

- Mingling personal with business financials

- Not providing for your own compensation from the business's revenue

- Mismanaging accounts receivable

- Thinking you can handle aspects of your business for which you don't have adequate training

- Micromanaging

Now let's take each threat in turn and see what you can do to prevent or minimize it.

Not enough cash reserves? Even if your business is relatively inexpensive to crank up, you probably will need to invest in its set-up, and then it may be several fiscal quarters (or more) before you are able to realize steady income (to say nothing of profits) for the company. Starting up with an adequate operating cash reserve will be your redeemer. This is one of many problems that a well-thought-out business plan should highlight. Don't fool yourself by wishfully thinking the money will somehow be there.

Plastic-dependent? Some small business owners are forced to turn to credit cards for early-stage survival, especially when they haven't planned properly. Credit cards carry high interest charges and sometimes annual fees. Whether it be through a small business loan, a capital infusion by outside investors or even your own personal funding, making sure there is sufficient operating capital can save you from getting into credit card debt. Avoid these unnecessary debits and use your cash.

Mixing personal and business finances? It can be tempting to cross the line between personal and business funds, especially in a one-person business. But it can lead to trouble, including shorting yourself or losing personal money if your business is in tough shape. Keeping these two entities completely separate not only makes it easier for accounting, budgeting and reconciling both sets of books, but it assists in determining your actual profits (or losses) for the small business. Your bank, investors, and tax authorities will want (or require) this practice anyway.

Shorting yourself on compensation? Throughout the early stages of your business's existence, it may seem like a solid decision to redistribute any and all your profits back into your business. This is an admirable, heroic point of view. However, not compensating yourself along the way could harm your personal finances and financial good standing. It's important to find the right balance for your specific personal needs. Once again, your business plan should show both your compensation and how it's going to be paid, particularly in the early period. Not budgeting early for this properly can lead to a personal financial problem.

Accounts receivable out of control? This is always a huge challenge for small business owners. Your payment terms should be printed on the back of every invoice, and you should have a clear process that you follow religiously in collecting payments. Hopefully, most of your top customers have a solid history of payment, but even they can have cash flow problems that cause them to make late or partial payments. A prompt reminder when a payment is not received on time can become part of the way you do business—after all, you are due that money. You can decide if imposing late fees or credit limits will work for both you and your customers.

Another serious risk in this area is becoming dependent on just a few customers, or having one giant customer and other little ones. If something happens to these key customers, you are in trouble. Allowing your best customers preferential payment terms is absolutely acceptable, as long as you can plan for it and the trade-off is reciprocated by real benefits to your business. If for some reason accounts receivable are mounting up (due to seasonal or other factors), it is reassuring if you have a cash reserve to draw on as an emergency back-up.

Need professional expertise? Knowing what you don't know applies particularly to certain aspects of business. As an entrepreneur, it is impossible to know the ins and outs of every legal, accounting, technology and industry issue. Tapping the expertise and experience of professionals in these and other specialized fields is both smart and safe. Professional advice may cost a good deal initially, but over the long haul, this guidance will keep you ahead of the curve in every aspect of your growing business. Budget for these needs and avoid even more financial pitfalls that could arise from attempting to do things you are not prepared to do professionally.

Micromanaging? This practice has its roots in the same soil as the threat we just looked at (thinking you know everything). Trying to do everything yourself and needlessly overseeing others prevent you from running your company at optimum levels. Trust your outsourced professionals, employees, freelancers and anyone else involved in your business affairs to do *their* job and you will succeed. Chances are if you chose these individuals correctly, they will do a better job than you anyhow. This is a good practice to follow from Day 1 because as your business grows, it will become impossible to micromanage your business anyway. Therefore avoid this trap early on by budgeting for it and giving people room to perform.

A few more things to consider

There are countless other pitfalls lurking out there. The ones we've just examined can be skirted if you keep your radar tuned for signs that one of them is looming ahead. But there are others that especially affect first-time entrepreneurs: opening too much credit early on, overinvesting too much in your business before it has proven itself, expanding too quickly, not paying attention to your financials and ledger sheets, and not staying completely organized in every aspect of your business. Surrounding yourself with a strong team of individuals internally and externally will go a long way in preventing these things from taking root and becoming a problem.

Starting a new business can be as rewarding as anything anybody looking for a challenge could hope for in life. Learning about potential financial pitfalls should never make you waver from your goal of becoming a successful entrepreneur either. In fact, it should help in validating your decision by instilling a higher degree of confidence in yourself. Navigating the whitewater of a start-up can even be fun. Just make sure to identify, document and learn from every step of your progress, including the financial pitfalls you encounter, and success will follow.

Ten Tax Mistakes to Avoid

They say nothing's surer than death and taxes.
Reduce the possibilities of tax problems by
avoiding these typical tax mistakes.

TAX ISSUES PRESENT an ever-changing, ongoing challenge to small business-es, particularly start-ups. They require consistent, competent attention and compliance. As we have seen, you simply must have access to a qualified professional tax advisor to prevent problems and avoid penalties.

The first two big mistakes

Yet even if you have a tax advisor, you need to keep a sharp eye on all your business's tax-related activity. Always ask questions and understand the reasons for the important decisions and choices you and your advisor take related to your overall tax strategies, as well as your tax planning, filings, credits, and so forth. After all, you know your business best. Your tax advisor is an expert in tax prac-tices, not your specific business sector, and certainly not your particular business. You must supply the context and rationales for the actions you take.

So that's the first mistake entrepreneurs make: **not being properly briefed and failing to understand the impact of important decisions related to taxes.** The good news is that if you address this need, you can avoid making most of the other common mistakes below. Just make sure you are fully briefed and that you understand what your advisor's strategy is for optimizing tax planning.

The second common mistake is **trying to save money by handling too many tax-related activities inside your company.** You certainly can process a lot of the basics internally, but even there, it pays to have your tax advisor help you set up and periodically review your day-to-day practices and systems (includ-ing your accounting software) so you capture and record all relevant data in an orderly way.

Other mistakes

- **Being ignorant about the current tax laws.** This is an easy way to get into trouble with your tax authority and incur significant fines and penalties.

- **Missing out on tax credits.** Changes in tax credit policies can appear or vanish for different reasons at different times. These need to be researched and pursued when they apply to your business.

- **Using wrong forms or handling things wrongly.** Certain filing requirements related to the use of specific forms, methods of reporting, reporting deadlines, and other specific information requirements are easy to miss, as are simple math or typing errors. Once you get off track or behind with reporting requirements, it can be very difficult to straighten out and clear up your data. The cost of bringing a professional in to clean up significant errors, incomplete filings, or missing reports will be significantly greater than the cost of using that resource from the beginning.

Once you have committed to using an appropriate resource to guide this process, there are a number of actions you must focus on to avoid tax mistakes caused by your own action or inaction. The primary mistakes that are within your control are these:

- **Insufficient or unacceptable documentation of business expenses.** This can be a real challenge. Your tax professional will rely on your records to substantiate any tax deductions or credits you might be claiming. This includes business travel, business entertainment, equipment purchases, disposable items purchased for the business, and other business-related expenses.

- **Proper information and details related to new hires.** The constantly changing tax laws in your area may offer specific tax credits or call for tax payments for employees who fit certain profiles. They may be related to military service, disability, demographics, the nature of your industry, or your business category.

- **Determining whether individuals working for you should be categorized as independent contractors or employees of the company.** You need to know the requirements for employment status and the corresponding employee benefit and tax withholding obligations. If you choose to engage the activities of an individual or a business as an independent contractor providing services to your business, it will be important to follow the appropriate guidelines for your area, and to meet all reporting and tax filing requirements. The key in this regard is to understand the specific regulations and reporting requirements in your area to understand when someone can be treated as an independent contractor, and when they must be treated as an employee of the company. Significant fines and penalties may be imposed if you do not comply with the specific guidelines for your business.

- **Not properly separating the business funds from personal funds in your records or bank accounts**. We mentioned this earlier, in connection with "good housekeeping" practices for your financials in general. Regarding taxes, though, if you aren't careful, funds can become co-mingled. If that happens, the legitimate tax deductions or tax credits you might qualify for may be disqualified because you did not maintain a clear and distinct business record for all financial transactions. Fines and penalties for this error vary, depending on where your business is located.

- **Not treating larger cash transactions in your business properly**. Recording cash transactions properly in your business accounting may not be enough to eliminate cash reporting mistakes. Sometimes a business that operates with a significant percentage of cash transactions may not correctly report all the activity in their accounting. The challenge comes when you organize expenses for tax reporting. Your expense/revenue ratios may not match those that your tax officials expect to see. This may raise a red flag that triggers a more detailed audit to identify additional specific details that may be incorrect. It pays to be well-informed and very precise about your obligations in this area, as in some countries, laws require separate and specific reporting for large cash transactions. (This requirement is being enforced more and more frequently as it can be a tool for identifying potential terrorist, drug, or other illegal activities.)

The moral of the story? Avoid making the most common business tax mistakes by finding a qualified tax professional to help you set up and maintain everything related to taxes. With proper tax planning, reporting and paying, you can rest assured that your business will be in excellent shape in the event the tax authorities raise any questions. Your partnership with a tax planning professional, including your efforts to ask questions, get fully briefed, and document and execute your tax practices correctly, has major implications. Why? Because as a business owner, even if you are not the person who makes a particular mistake, you are the one who will held responsible.

M.O.

CHAPTER V

Day-to-Day Financing

Why Cash is King

*Unlike in a chess game, in finance, this King
is the most versatile and easy to maneuver.
It's about liquidity.*

HAVE YOU ever heard the expression "Cash is King"? I heard it in business classes and around the office for a while before I really understood what it meant. You've probably guessed that it either means that *money* is king—in the sense that it makes the world go 'round—or that compared to other forms of business assets, paper money is king because it's the easiest to convert into other things—equipment, investment accounts, expansion, tools, etc.

Although we talk about *cash* in everyday conversation to mean the wad of bills you carry around in your wallet or purse, for accountants and financial professionals it means your *currency (including coins) on hand, bank account balances, negotiable money orders and checks.* And, my friends, this kind of cash is king because it's the most flexible form of asset and is the easiest to work with. It's liquid. In general, if you have cash in your possession, you can always do something with it immediately, if the need arises.

Cash is important to businesses and especially to start-ups, for several reasons. As you probably don't have a wealth of financial assets when you're trying to start a new business, it is in your best interest to stretch those coins and make them count. With cash, you can purchase assets to run your business, pay employees, pay bills and other expenses, etc. without finance charges. The best part about cash is that if you have it, you clearly don't have to wait for it to come in. That sounds a little silly, but let me explain....

Imagine that you've recently started a business. You've built it from the ground up and have already hired an employee to assist in the growth and development of your new business. You even have a few regular customers who love your product and pay their bills promptly at the end of every month. You're confident that your customers will keep bringing you their business, so toward the beginning of the month, you decide to go out and purchase new computers and printers for yourself and your employee to use for work. You want them to last for a while so you buy the top-of-the-line equipment. Since you trust that your customers will pay their bills at the end of the month, you aren't uncomfortable using up the last of the cash in your monthly operating budget, since you paid all your bills on the first of the month. You did, however, remember to leave enough money in the operating account to pay yourself and your employee on the fifteenth of the month.

When you return to your office—in a funky old warehouse that you paid very little for—you walk in the door to a swampy mess all over the floor. Your tiny bathroom has flooded, leaving your office a horrible mess. You discover it will cost quite a bit to repair the pipe, get the floor cleaned up, and replace the carpet. And all the cleaning and carpet companies in your area only take cash. What are you going to do now? It's too big a mess to try to tackle yourself. You can't afford to get it cleaned up without spending the cash you allocated to your salaries, and you and your employee can't afford to miss a paycheck.

This story could go on and on but the basic concept is already clear. If you can, always retain a cushion of cash resources. Why? Because cash is king. Some businesses don't extend lines of credit, some don't accept personal checks or credit cards, and some still don't accept wire transfers. Truthfully, most businesses accept all of those things, but they charge a premium for processing and it often takes time to process, sometimes several days. The bottom line is that cash is king because everybody accepts it. And if you have it, you can use it immediately.

In fact, there are benefits for people who are willing to pay cash. During the handful of financial crises over the past century, cash became the leader in financial transactions because there was no need for any trust behind it. As the markets dipped, "I promise to pay" carried less and less weight. What businesses wanted was cash (paper currency), certified check, or direct transfer. In fact, most financial crises of the last century could be credited to people and businesses saying that they could afford to pay for things that they really couldn't. They didn't actually have the cash they claimed they had to back up their purchases. They defaulted on payments and that was that.

So cash is king because it's there when we need it and it keeps us honest. In a world dominated by leverage, payables, receivables, etc., still the only real guarantee to fiscal stability is having cash. If you're starting a business or growing a new one, always ensure that you have cash resources available.

S.G.

The True Cost of Money and Opportunity

Numbers aren't always evident, especially when you need to finance some of your activity.

MOST SMALL BUSINESS OWNERS and entrepreneurs know that money isn't free. But many don't recognize that even when you have capital resources (money in some form) at your disposal, those resources have an opportunity cost.

Cost of money and opportunity costs

Given that your resources are limited, you will frequently have to make choices between two or more ways to spend a sum of money. Your opportunity cost in these situations is the cost of passing up the next-best cost when choosing between two or more alternative expenses.

Unless you are a large bank in the U.S. and it's back to 2011, then you probably don't have access to interest-free capital (Ha-Ha!). Most of us, in our personal lives and in business, rely on borrowing needed funds from a lender like a bank or credit card company. These capital resources are usually lent to a borrower at a certain interest rate and repayment term. You may think, "What's the big deal? Why do I care about 6, 7 or 8 percent interest, or even 15 percent interest?"

Well then, answer is simple: When you're dealing with a very small amount of money, or a small amount with respect to the size and scope of your project, over a short period of time, then in fact it may not matter a lot. However, if you begin to grow and you start dealing in larger amounts as your equipment needs increase, your material supplies grow, etc., you may begin to notice a financial "sucking sound." This is the proverbial drain working hard on your operating account. These types of expense can just kill a business without the owner even being aware of it.

Also, these types of circumstances commonly affect seasonal and cyclical businesses, no matter whether they are manufacturing companies, wholesalers, distributors or retailers. It doesn't matter. The cost of money and the opportunity cost of money still exist.

Opportunity costs made simple

What about those opportunity costs? Business owners have a hard time admitting to the opportunity costs they have incurred by making certain decisions. Think about this for a second.

Let's say your company really should exhibit at a trade show that has an exhibition fee of U.S. $2,500. But instead you decide to buy a much-needed new laptop for the company. The average person might say, "So what? I would have spent $2,500 either way, and I chose to buy the laptop over attending the show. Big deal." However, this thinking is far from correct.

The actual ramifications of the choice may never be known, but we can loosely estimate them. Let's say you skipped going to the trade show. That would have cost $2,500. So you didn't pay that out. But by not going to the trade show you also didn't attend any of the keynote presentations or workshops, potentially missing out on cutting-edge industry information and insight. Now what was the value of all of that information that you also by-passed?

Moving on, what about all of the relationships, business or otherwise, that may have come from you participating at the event? How many new contacts would you have made? How many of those contacts and relationships could have become new customers or could have referred you to new customers? And as a last and most important question: How much new business could have been generated by the industry information, contacts, relationships and referrals you would have accumulated from the trade show?

If you answer all of those questions and add up all of the values and potential revenues, you now have the opportunity cost of that $2,500 computer. If you take that probably extremely large number and add in the $2,500 you spent on the computer, you will have its true cost! It's crazy when you see what you really spent. Really.

Cost of money counts

Now that we've explained opportunity cost in a very basic way, let's shed some light on how the cost of money can really sneak up on a growing business.

Let's say you are a small business, manufacturing a product halfway around the world for sale in your home market to wholesalers and distributors there. You have done all of the necessary legwork and you've been successful at creating a replacement widget to serve an already existing demand for a large wholesaler or distributor. You think you're doing well. Maybe you took in a few million in revenue last year, your business is growing nicely, and you are on your way.

Now you've built this great new product and you have found a buyer. The buyer represents 800 retail stores and they want 20 units in each store right away. These units cost you roughly $62.50 and but your client has every intention of selling these units for $200. His number may not be important, but your cost is. Now, you will be lucky if the buyer is willing to put any money down (i.e., pre-pay a portion of the invoice upon ordering). Most of these buyers want favorable terms or they want you to store the product in your warehouse and pay you as it comes off your shelves. But, let's assume you are a great negotiator and the buyer wants and needs your product. She agrees to pay you 25% down, with her order, but the rest is net 30 (the remainder of the invoice is due 30 days after delivery).

So you speak to the factory in that distant land. They say the cost to produce your 16,000 total units at $62.50 is $1,000,000. As you know, your customer has agreed to pay you 25 percent with her order, but the factory wants 50 percent pre-paid to start production and the remaining 50 percent F.O.B. (Freight On Board). That means the factory gets the rest of their money before the ship leaves with the product for your warehouse.

What do you do? Well, you will have to first fully understand the timeline for payments between all parties involved, plus production time and shipping. Let's say production takes eight weeks, then shipping on a cargo ship takes five weeks to the port nearest you, then one week on a dedicated truck to your facility, then five more days to get from your warehouse to the buyer. Then there are 30 more days until you receive the remainder of your invoiced amount.

All in all, that process takes approximately four to five months in total. You had to pay the factory $500,000 up front and the remaining $500,000 when the vendor loaded the goods on the boat, three months before you would get paid the balance due from your customer.

What do you do? Let's keep the math simple. One approach is to take out two loans. You could borrow $250,000, then come back 45 days later and borrow another $500,000. But you would have to pay a second round of loan origination fees that way. Instead, you would most likely take out one loan or line of credit after you collected $250,000 from the buyer. So you would have to borrow 750,000 from a lender for 5 months. Following me?

Suppose you borrow $750,000 at 8 percent interest annually. This means that just your interest expense for borrowing the money is $25,000. *Most entrepreneurs fail to account for this additional expense when pricing the product for the buyer.*

I've seen businesses attempt to operate on razor-thin margins and accidentally contractually commit to supply product at a price that causes them to lose money! How crazy is that! In this example you would have to add approximately $1.57 to the $62.50 to cover your interest on your loan, which is your "True Cost of Money," making the actual sale price to the buyer $64.07.

The Annoying Ambiguity of Business Banking

As Bob Hope once said, "A bank will only lend you money once you can prove that you don't need it."

THIS SIMPLE YET BRILLIANT quote sums up the banking experience for all entrepreneurs and small business owners. Banks and their loan officers love to give a borrower's leash a strong yank the minute business financials fall below expectations, or if receivables experience a downturn.

But what about an entrepreneur's strategic efforts to grow a business via actions that temporarily depress short-term performance, or even growth? For example, let's say you own a manufacturing plant, and your team has recently developed a new product with lower material costs, lower production costs, a higher gross margin and some sort of new competitive edge in the form of performance, market interest or innovation.

There is just one problem. Your plant is only so big, you're limited on labor resources and you are hoping to replace an older, antiquated product line with the new one. Now you've made the choice to shut down the old line, retool that portion of the facility and make ready for larger volume and better quality control. But in doing so, you are incurring some irregular additional expenses as well as strategically shutting down a percentage of your regular revenue, causing you to run in the red for a short time. Your banker will flip, and most likely ask that you reduce your loan balance, if not pay it off, unless you can collateralize the line with PLENTY of assets. And presto! You've just proven Bob Hope was right.

As entrepreneurs and business owners, we often look at things with a polar opposite viewpoint from bankers. They love the TTM (Trailing Twelve Months) measuring stick. For them, everything is based on mitigating risk. That's why past performance is the most common tool used by lenders when they review your current performance and future forecasts and projections.

We entrepreneurs see risk as a necessity for growth and expansion. As Jack Welch, former CEO of GE once said, "If you're not constantly innovating and finding new ways to grow, you're already dead." This is why most entrepreneurs and small businesses that are in the ever-so-fun start-up phase tend to rely on personal lines of credit, friends, family, and private or angel investors rather than traditional lending resources such as banks and credit unions.

Crowd funding

One common misconception is that as a business owner looking to raise funds, you seek out only one or two individuals that could potentially provide the necessary capital for the project. If you take this route, it's not bad, and it may be all the financing you will ever need. So if it's easy to access, then great. Go ahead and get started. However, for those of us who may need multiple rounds of funding to grow the business to a certain size and scale, it may be smart to raise smaller amounts of funding from a larger, broader group of funders. This is sometimes called crowd funding.

Like anything, crowd funding has its advantages and disadvantages. Obviously, if you draw funds from a larger number of backers, you will multiply the time you spend on "investor relations," e.g., calling, meeting, presenting and closing. But there's a potential pay-back in this. If you can successfully spread the "raise" over a multitude of investors, and specifically those will lower net worth, you may be able to leverage these relationships in the future. If later you need additional capital, you can explain the risks of not re-investing to keep the business alive—and also keep their investments alive.

Now, we're not urging you to raise money from those who can't afford it or to mislead anyone on the prospective success of your business. We are simply saying that an individual with a higher net worth could provide a first round of funding to get you going, but later, if you need more money to grow or to finish the launch, build out, etc., hold back on investing additional funds. In these circumstances, a higher-net-worth individual may just say no thanks, accept the loss and most likely write it off at tax time.

Some countries have regulations that control the number of investors that companies with a particular type of business structure can work with. For example, in the U.S., Limited Liability Companies (LLCs) can only have up to 100 investor members. Therefore, if you are based in the U.S. and anticipating more members/ equity partners, etc., then you may need to choose a different type of business structure. It's best to get professional advice on matters like this.

I once knew a gentleman who had a long-standing relationship with a bank in his home town. This gentleman's business was founded by his father decades prior. After assuming control of the family business and growing it significantly, the gentleman decided to take out a loan to "grow the business." Because this was years ago, he simply collateralized the loan with his business and its assets, something most business owners would think twice about doing (in case they couldn't pay the loan back and would lose the business to the bank). The borrower then decided to issue himself a few bonuses over the next few years, while meanwhile the business suffered. Eventually, the business could no longer service the note and the owner defaulted. But that was okay with this individual. He happily gave the bank "the keys" and moved on with his millions in bonuses. No wonder banks are pretty serious in sizing up the risks they face when issuing a loan!

Just remember, if you are lacking credit, personal capital resources and/or collateral, then traditional bank issued debt financing probably won't work. It is common nowadays for a bank to obtain personal guarantees and other types of collateralization in an effort to mitigate any or all of the risk associated with business lending. So think creatively when you go after funding and shake the money tree with care.

LIFO vs. FIFO

If you're a fan of the Marx brothers, you might think
LIFO and FIFO are sisters of Groucho, Harpo,
Chico, Gummo and Zeppo. No way!

IF YOUR COMPANY DEALS IN GOODS, you need to get familiar with the LIFO and FIFO accounting methods and, depending on where you are based, decide which one is best for tracking and accounting for your inventory and the cost of goods you have sold. There are two methods: *Last-In, First-Out* (LIFO) and *First-In, First-Out* (FIFO). The names refer to the way you assign value to your stock on hand (your unsold inventory) in your bookkeeping. And as their names suggest, LIFO considers that the latest stock to arrive in inventory is the first sold, while FIFO assumes the oldest stock gets sold first.

A number of variables are important to consider. But before we take a look at them, we want to point out that this is certainly an issue you'll want advice on from your accountant. So read on in the spirit of getting yourself up to speed for that conversation, not to take a decision based only on what you read here.

FIFO and LIFO basics

The primary issues to consider when evaluating these two methods of inventory accounting are:

- the impact to your business for the value of unsold inventory

- the cost of goods sold (COGS)

- the fact that both GAAP and IFRS accounting standards support the FIFO method, but IFRS standards do not permit LIFO (we'll decipher that in a moment!)

If your business is based in the United States, your accountant follows GAAP: Generally Accepted Accounting Principles. It's a set of rules that govern how your accounting data is created and reported. A second system, used in 110 countries, including those in the European Union, is called the International Financial Reporting Standard (IFRS). It's based more on principles that you and your accountant can apply in your accounting activities. The U.S. Securities and Exchange Commission (SEC) currently uses GAAP, but plans call for a convergence between GAAP and IFRS by 2015. The importance of the foregoing is that both GAAP and IFRS permit FIFO, while LIFO is not permitted in IFRS-bound countries. In short, if you live in an IFRS country, you only really need to read half of this section!

Applying the principles and rules

Imagine a stack of goods arrives in your warehouse on Day 2 of your business. You ordered them on Day 1 at a certain price per unit, so they have a certain total value. One month later, you've sold half of them and re-ordered stock. It turns out that the new stock costs more, or less, per unit than your initial stock. So you add those goods to the top of your stack. What's the value of that stack? Do you average the cost of goods? Do you sell your old, first stock first, or your new, restock first? How will your choice affect your tax bill and your profit? These are the questions that LIFO and FIFO address.

Obviously, value you assign to your unsold inventory and/or COGS *will* have a direct impact on your company's profitability and tax liability. In order to get the big picture about how to determine the impact of LIFO vs. FIFO inventory accounting for your stock, we will walk you through three examples.

Example 1—The Shoe Store

Let's suppose you are starting a shoe store. And suppose that each pair of shoes you buy as your start-up stock will cost less than the ones you'll be buying next year as replenishment stock, due to inflation, increasing labor and transport costs, etc. In this case, your "First In" shoes cost less than the identical "Last In" inventory you will buy next year.

If you are tracking inventory using FIFO, you are selling the lowest COGS first and maintaining the highest potential profit. The value of your ending-period inventory will be the highest as well, because it is the most recently acquired at the highest cost.

If, however, you are using LIFO for inventory accounting, you are selling the highest COGS first and achieving the lowest profit margin. The value of your ending-period inventory will be the lowest because it was purchased at the oldest and lowest cost.

Example 2—The News Stand

Suppose now that you are opening a tiny news stand outside a train station. Your business plan calls for you to start out buying a small number of copies of each magazine and newspaper you will sell to begin with, but due to your marketing efforts, you can expect to purchase higher volumes per item after the first three months. And you feel confident and that you'll continue increasing your orders each quarter there-after for two years. Your suppliers offer better pricing based on the volume you buy, so you can plan on *decreasing* your per-unit costs of goods over time. Therefore your *First-In* newspapers and magazines will cost *more* than the *Last-In* items.

If you are using FIFO inventory accounting here, you are selling the highest COGS first and achieving the lowest profit margin. The value of your ending-period inventory will be the lowest as well, because it is the most recently acquired at the lowest cost.

If, however, you are using LIFO for inventory accounting, you are selling the lowest COGS first and maintaining the highest profit margin. The value of your ending-period inventory will be the highest as well, because it was purchased at the oldest and highest cost.

Example 3: Comparing the impact of the two methods

In an article entitled "Rules for Changing From FIFO to LIFO," John Cromwell of Demand Media makes an elegantly simple calculation.*

> To illustrate the difference in methods, assume that you started your business this year with no inventory and acquired three lots of goods during the financial year. The first 1,000 units cost $3, the second lot of 1,000 cost $2 and the last lot cost $3. Prior to this year, you had no inventory. If you sold 2,500 units, your ending inventory balance per LIFO would be $1,500 and $500 under FIFO.

Financial reporting strategies

If your company's location allows you to choose between FIFO and LIFO, then based on the primary audience you need to address, there may be financial reporting strategies that influence your choice. The first step is to identify who your primary audience is for your company's financial reporting. Once you know that, you will be able to determine the method of inventory accounting that best reports the targets they are expecting you to meet. For example,

- Tax liabilities may vary, depending on the location of your business, the structure of the business's ownership, *and* your inventory accounting.

- Lenders may place specific performance requirements on the busi-nesses that favor one method over the other.

- Investors and investor analysts may have certain expectations for your company's financial performance over a specific period of time that matches best with one or the other method as well.

*See http://smallbusiness.chron.com/rules-changing-fifo-lifo-36595.html.

In addition, there may be an audience for a period of time that prefers to pursue *lower* inventory levels and *lower* tax liabilities because of a specific financial or tax plan. There could be lenders that require *maximum* inventory value and *maximum* profitability for the immediate period to establish confidence for a major capital funding or refinance initiative.

And in case you're wondering if you can hop back and forth between the methods, either from year to year or from product to product, the simple answer is "No, not easily," and sometimes just "No." Again, consult with your accountant to get complete, specific answers.

Tracking and reporting issues

Another factor that enters into this discussion is your available resources for inventory accounting. The LIFO method can often lead to some significantly aged inventory items that you need to track and report on for an extended period of time. This becomes more complex than the FIFO method, where there is much less aging of inventory. If your business has lots of individual items that need tracking and you have limited bookkeeping resources, FIFO might make more sense, all things considered.

Market issues

Your choice of method will also come into play as you monitor and forecast the economic stability of your business sector and the overall market. In a more stable market, the LIFO vs. FIFO choice is pretty straightforward. The complexity comes in when you consider the dynamics of international business and the international economy.

If your business is locally focused (say, you grow tomatoes for the local farmer's market), you should be pretty well insulated from global situations and your accounting decision will be fairly obvious. But if your business buys and/or sells internationally, things get more complex. The impact of inflation on your COGS coming from one part of the world may be completely different than a deflationary impact to your selling price in a different international market. Your strategy about where you purchase and where you sell internationally may show very different results, depending on your method on inventory accounting. Also, if you picked your method of inventory accounting to be consistent with a specific financial goal, you must closely monitor and adjust international purchasing sources and customer sales outlets that respond to changes in inflationary or deflationary impacts to your plan.

It is important to remember that the method of inventory accounting you use is a tool that reports financial information in a specific way. So work closely with your accountant to determine both your strategy and the method that works best for you.

Trade Show Tips and Tricks

Many business people think trade shows are still worth attending, even in our digital era. The associated costs, however, can kill you. Think smart if you exhibit.

AS COMMERCE is conducted more and more via the Internet, people question the value of attending or exhibiting at conferences and expos in their business sectors. So much of it is just schmoozing and hype, or dry slide shows in drafty ballrooms. If you are in a line of business that features an annual or seasonal event, you'll need to decide if it's smart to be there. The math is not just about money.

Despite the digital marketplace, many feel that the chance to meet, talk, snoop, and even do business is still worth it. Before you make an impulsive decision, write down a specific list of goals you hope to achieve by going. Get the full costs: travel, lodging, entertainment, space, décor, materials, time spent away from the office, and anything else that applies. Then ask yourself if you think you'll make enough back (in orders or connections or visibility or whatever) to justify the time and expense. And look into cheaper ways of attending, like renting a table or panel in the small business section, sharing space with a compatible company, etc. If you've never attended before, maybe just walking the show this year will help you decide what to do in the future.

I'm not trying to bash conventions, trade shows, or the invaluable support required from countless services and hard-working people when operating every facet of a trade show, convention or symposium. However, I want to offer vitally important information regarding the hidden costs of exhibiting at these events. As an entrepreneur or small business owner, you may not have been involved in the financial planning or bill-paying associated with such events.

- Do not scan—READ CAREFULLY—through exhibitor paperwork, set-up regulations, or any other documentation pertaining to the event before you sign up. Last year, it cost one of us *less* to fly round trip, halfway across the U.S. and back, to attend a trade show than it cost to have the television we rented for the show pushed on a cart for 200 yards (or meters) from storage to our exhibit space. We were victims of hidden mandatory labor charges, wouldn't you say?

- Sometimes, it actually isn't the exhibit space or the trade show booth that is the most expensive. Depending on the show location, a business can spend more money on mandatory set-up fees, handling charges, delivery expenses, disposal, carpet, etc., than they would ever reasonably expect. Be aware that moving in equipment, renting it, even the tape you buy to pack up boxes afterward are outrageously overpriced.

- And if you're thinking, "I'll just carry my own TV!" No, you won't. Because the fine print in your exhibitor contract prohibits that.

So what's the answer? When attending shows that allow for some flexibility, try a few simple steps:

- Find out if you can carry items for your exhibit space. Quite often, the mandatory labor fees only apply to items that cannot be carried by one person or to items that require the use of the venue's loading dock.

- Next, research different exhibit tools that can be broken down and carried. There are numerous trade show resources that specialize in lightweight marketing aids such as stands, banners and booth enhancements that come with special carrying cases that can be checked as luggage or brought onboard as a carry-on. This can save a small business a ton of money over time, especially if the business plans on exhibiting at multiple shows during a year.

- If you decide to follow the tips above and ship items to the location ahead of time to avoid the hassle, simply call your hotel—"Good morning, this is (Your Name) with (Company Name) and I will be arriving on (Date/Time). I was wondering if I could send a package to myself, ahead of time." They will likely say, "No problem. We can hold it in our luggage room." This is extremely helpful because now, even if you splurge for shipping, you can still save on the handling charges found at most venues. Just take your package with you to the exhibit hall and carry it in on your own. That could pay for your plane ticket!

And now a word about trade show etiquette and follow-up. All of this seems blindingly obvious, but you'd be surprised at how many exhibitors fail to do the simple things that can make attending pay off.

- Ensure that your personnel at your exhibit know their job is to greet attendees and present your offering, not catch up on emails, eat lunch, or joke around with each other like they're on vacation. Make clear what the dress code will be, have a schedule of who covers what and when, and line up your appointments well in advance, also allowing time (if possible) to cruise around and collect industry intelligence.

- Equip everyone with suitable meeting report forms (which could be templates in their laptops or tablets) that clearly capture the essentials of each meeting and define what and when the follow-ups are. After saying goodbye, your colleague should mark a priority code on each form for post-show processing.

- When you get back to the office, debrief and make follow-up lists. Continue to meet regularly to review progress (and dead ends) for all the leads you identified.

- If you want, you can chart what business you won, what contacts you made or made new progress with, etc. and monetize the results. That will help you determine whether it was a good investment to attend and make it easy to decide whether to do it again next year.

In the end, the message is simple. Industry events are often hugely beneficial and can be a great source for leads, relationships and education. Run a trade show appearance as a marketing campaign with its own P&L, then plan and execute your campaign accordingly. And go for it!

M.O.

Time Is Money—How to Get More of Both

*Efficiency, smart prioritizing, discipline and focus
are best practices for financial success.*

IN DAILY BUSINESS, there are always reports, charts, spreadsheets, emails, meetings and other things that can consume significant hours of your day if you let them dictate where you focus your mind and energy. The key to effectively managing your daily business is to correctly identify the most important pieces of information you need to monitor, and to organize a method for handling and acting on that information daily. After all, time *is* money.

That's why it is all about being efficient and focused. The financial success of your business radiates from the efficiency of your own daily routine. Your work habits for optimizing your phone for calls and texting, handling email, conducting or attending meetings and exchanging information set the tone and present an example for your associates. It's essential to be well-organized and efficient, beginning with your daily routine.

An effective business manager also knows how to distinguish between those issues and events that are merely *important* from those that are truly *urgent*. It is far too easy to be drawn into the vortex of apparently urgent things which pull you off course, away from items you know you should have focused on first.

So do a little self-assessment, starting with a diagnosis of your current state. For several days, log your work life. Begin each day with a specific to-do list for the day. Note what you do with your time, roughly hour by hour. At the end of the day, total up the time you spent on various categories of activity: sending or reading emails; talking or texting by phone; sitting in meetings; searching the web; entertaining; preparing for upcoming events; and creating, reading or reviewing various reports. Compare your actual activity and results with your planned activity and goals for that day and give yourself a score. You may be surprised to learn how much time you spent doing things that sabotage your daily plan.

As you go through this exercise you will identify time wasters, those unproductive activities and habits that keep you from effectively leading, monitoring and managing the relevant drivers of your business. Are you writing long, vague emails that require cycles of back-and-forth clarifications? Are you micro-managing or not delegating effectively? Do you know how to get the most from the software tools you use? The challenge is to eliminate these obstacles. There are books, workshops, online courses and consultants who can help you develop or improve disciplined, efficient work habits. You probably have a few that work for you already, but you can always gain from fresh ideas and techniques.

And by the way, if your work log exercise reveals that you are indeed micro-managing, putting off decisions, and if you feel frustrated, overwhelmed, exhausted, scared or pessimistic, ask yourself if you are suffering from burn-out. It could be that your inefficiencies are tied to this common threat to entrepreneurs. We can't get into a long discussion of burn-out and how to deal with it here, but we suggest that if you suspect that's part of your picture, you deal with it as well as seeking to improve your work and thinking habits. You can find help in books, online, and from consultants and coaches. One quick tip: try to STOP, then CHALLENGE, then FOCUS to break out of the burn-out trap.

Work habits per se can only take you so far. In addition, you must develop the habit of focusing on the key drivers and goals of your business and relentlessly give them your top priority attention. You actually can afford to skim semi-important documents, not attend every meeting you are invited to, and dismiss non-essential matters that have less impact on your business. Knowing how many office supplies your company uses daily is far less important than knowing how many key products were sold and at what profit margin.

By developing these efficiencies and prioritizing ruthlessly, you will both free up time and become a better strategist and manager. That will directly and indirectly impact your business financially. You will want to check on certain key drivers every day, even if on some days you merely glance at the bottom line or scan an online report. Make yourself a list of the things that fall into this category. It may include:

- Sales and profit margins

- Inventory and production planning

- Labor (hours worked, capacity, productivity, etc.)

- Receivables

- Payables

- Human resource and employee issues

- Bank, tax and other financial issues or data

- External factors that affect your business (weather, current events, industry trends, etc.)

- Planning

- A weather forecast: is there anything brewing or exploding that needs your immediate attention which is not covered in the rest of your key driver list?

When you have identified your key drivers, you can set up a disciplined daily regime that will help you manage your business's daily and longer-term performance. It will give you a far more pro-active point of view *plus* the time to plan and think as a business leader, rather than being an anxious hamster on a wheel. And as a bonus, the example you set with this approach will ripple out through your company's evolving culture, and will instill confidence, efficiency and pro-active thinking in your associates.

What is Your Business Really Worth?

*If you're planning on selling your business,
the first step is determining its value.*

FOR MANY ENTREPRENEURS, it's the start-up phase of business that they truly love (and often, are truly best at—these types are not so good at guiding the day-to-day, plodding growth that other entrepreneurs dream of). For others, the time has come to move on to another new venture, or to retire. And still others decide that running a business is just not for them. For these and a variety of other reasons, they all start thinking of selling their businesses.

But it's hard to start planning to sell if you don't know your company's worth. You need to have a notion of this number to be sure it's smart to sell. And of course you want to get a fair price for the business, according to its current market value. You hope to get enough money to help you make another investment, retire or move back into the life of an employee.

To learn the monetary value of your business, there are three techniques you can use.

- The first technique is dependent on your assets. This means that the value of your business may be equated to the value of your tangible assets. These include buildings, machinery, equipment, motor vehicles, and any other assets that your business owns.

- Another technique compares your business's profile with that of other similar businesses that have sold, and adjust for significant differences. For instance, there is a market value for coffee roasting businesses. If you own a coffee roasting business, your tangible assets may not be factored into the valuation, but instead, your annual sales, customer base, and so forth will be considered.

- The third technique is income-based. Your business will be valued according to how much income and profit it generates. The higher the income and profit, the higher the value will be.

One of the factors that may affect the value of your business is the number of years you have been in operation. A reputable, established business will sell for a lot more than a business that has only been in operation for a few months. If you have been operating the business for a number of years, you've likely developed a solid reputation in your area and industry. The reputation you have and the clientele you built all equate to value when it comes time to sell your business.

Depending on the nature of your business, you might be able to handle the sale yourself, or with the help of the attorney you have consulted with over time. Larger or more specialized businesses may be better off being sold via a business broker. Such a person can help establish a price and locate interested buyers for you.

Either way, you need to prepare up-to-date data about your company's performance, products or services, assets and employees. Gather all the records related to these things, including data on the number of employees you have and their levels of experience. This information, taken as a whole, will help establish the value of your business in the marketplace. In general, the higher the number of well-trained, highly qualified employees you have, the higher the value will be.

The extent and condition of all your assets will also affect your sales proposition of your business in the marketplace. If you have sophisticated, expensive, working machinery, the value of your business will be higher.

It is always good to ensure that all your machinery, equipment and company vehicles are serviced and in good working condition before you sell your business. If they are in poor condition, they may affect your ability to find buyers or reduce the amount of money that you will get from the sale. Ensure that you have proper documentation and sales agreements for your assets. If you have any standing manufacturer's warranties, provide these during the valuation process. In our digital age, proprietary software can be just as valuable as tangible property owned by the business.

More than the total assets and equipment your company has, however, it's your company's *performance* and *potential* that will make it valuable. A company that has lots of "stuff," isn't nearly as valuable as a company that is bringing in tons of money and can demonstrate upward trends in sales performance. The longer your company's trends, the safer, and thus the more valuable, your company will be to a buyer.

Internet businesses can be worth more than you'd ever imagine. When we first started ExpertBusinessAdvice.com, our web developer kept telling us about ways to increase our viewership and about the dramatic increase in our company's value we could get by increasing its volume of unique viewers (read: customers). In theory, for an Internet business, when it comes to marketing, people visiting your website are the same as people buying something from you. The trick is, though, they all have to be *different* people. You can't just have your 10 closest friends visit your website over and over all day long. Once we started focusing our marketing initiatives on bringing more people to the site, the value of ExpertBusinessAdvice.com skyrocketed, due to the mass influx of unique visitors.

Determining your business's worth is an intriguing exercise. A certain number of entrepreneurs go through it now and then, only to conclude that it's not the right time to sell, for any number of reasons. But you don't get to that fork in your decision path without knowing what price you can get for it, so it's a fruitful exercise, whatever the outcome.

Appendix: A Detailed View of How to Write a Business Plan*

Writing a business plan is the most important facet of starting a business.

AFTER YOU HAVE your big idea, the very next thing you should work on is your business plan. As we've seen, the business plan has several purposes. It captures your ideas on paper and keeps track of the steps you've taken or will take to start the business. It's also a major requirement in acquiring financing for your business. No one will want to help you start your business unless you can convince them that your plan will keep your business from crashing soon after takeoff.

Below, you will find a detailed guide for writing the sections that make up a basic business plan. We've written it with a funding request in mind; if you are creating your plan for your own reference, use your own judgment about the level of detail and items you include. Naturally, if you are writing your plan to test the idea of starting a certain business, you won't have any history to report either. It may help you to think of the project as writing several connected, self-contained reports.

* * *

The EXECUTIVE SUMMARY is the first part of a business plan and is the most crucial piece. It provides a very concise synopsis of the entire plan, along with a brief history of your company (if there is one). This portion tells readers what your business is or will be, and where you want to take it. It's the first thing your readers see; it will either grab their attention and make them want to keep learning, or make them want to close the cover and move on to something else. Most importantly, this part of the plan tells why you believe your business will be successful.

*This section first appeared in our book *A Crash Course in Starting a Business* (Nova Vista Publishing, ISBN 978-90-77256-36-7).

Here's a tip: The Executive Summary is most easily and effectively written after you finish writing the rest of your business plan. Once all of the details of your plan are in order, you will be prepared to condense it into the Executive Summary. Try to keep this section to fewer than four pages.

Included in the Executive Summary are:

- Mission Statement: The Mission Statement briefly explains the focus of your business. The statement can technically be any length, although we recommend shooting for two to three sentences. It should be as direct and concise as possible and it should leave the reader with a clear picture of what your business is all about.

- When the business was started

- Key management and their roles

- Number of employees

- Primary and other locations of the business

- Description of office, manufacturing plant, or facilities

- The products or services

- Current investor information and any additional financial relationships or arrangements

- Brief summary of your company's financial accomplishments and any noteworthy market activities (e.g., your business tripled its value in a one-year period or you became the leader in your industry by developing a certain product)

- Briefly describe management's plans for the business's future.

With the exception of the Mission Statement, the information in the Executive Summary should be presented in a brief or bulleted style. Note that this information is expanded upon in greater detail within the remainder of the business plan.

If you are just starting a business, you most likely will not have a lot of information to populate all the fields mentioned above. As an alternative, focus on your experience, background, and the decisions that led you to start the business. Ensure that it contains information about the needs your target market has and what solutions your business will provide. Explain how the business experience you have will allow you to make meaningful advances into the market. Point out what you're going to do uniquely or more effectively than your competition. Show that there is a definite need for the product or service provided by your business, then address the business's prospective plans.

To help the reader in pinpointing specific sections within your business plan, provide a table of contents immediately following the Executive Summary. The content titles should be very broad; try not to include too much detail.

* * *

The MARKET ANALYSIS portion is Part Two of a well-written business plan. It should demonstrate your knowledge of the particular industry that your business plans to enter. It should also provide basic statistics and key information of any market research data you have obtained. However, the itemized details of your market research studies should be placed in the Appendix section of the business plan.

This part of the business plan should include a description of the industry, target market facts and information, market test results, timeframes, and an evaluation of your competition.

The Industry Description section should include an overview of your primary industry: industry size, current and trailing growth rates, market trends and characteristics relating to the entire industry. What is the life-cycle stage of the industry? What is the industry's expected growth rate? It should profile the major customer groups within the industry (businesses, governments, women over 35 years of age, children under five, etc.). This can be broad or narrow, depending on the size and scope of the industry and the business you are in.

The business's target market is the customer base that it aims to supply products or provide services to. When defining a target market, it's vital to narrow the group to a realistic size. Often, businesses make the fatal miscalculation of trying to offer something to everybody. This approach typically ends in failure.

Within the Target Market section, you should report information that identifies the following:

- **Key characteristics** of the primary group you are targeting. This segment should include information about the critical needs of your future customers, the level to which those needs are currently being met, and the demographics of the group. Ensure you also include the geographic location of your target market; identify the key decision-makers, and any seasonal or cyclical trends that may impact the industry or your business model.

- **Size** of the target market. Here, you should report the number of potential customers in your primary market, the amount of annual purchases they make relative to products or services at par with your own, the geographic area they inhabit, and the expected market growth for this group.

- The **magnitude of market share** you expect to capture and the reasons why. When gathering this information, you need to decide how much market share and how many customers you expect to gain in a specific geographic region. In addition, you should provide the reader with an understanding of the reasoning you used in developing these estimates. Some businesses, for example day care centers, may be limited by law to the number of customers they can serve. Explain these things here if they apply.

- **Pricing and gross margin** expectations. In this section, it would be wise to define the structure of your pricing, your gross margin requirements, and any discounts or incentives that you plan to offer through the business, such as large-volume purchasing, bulk discounts, or prompt payment discounts that discourage customers from taking advantage of payment terms.

- A list of target market **research** and information sources. These resources can be purchased demographic research, directories, business associations, industry publications, and government documents. Or you can do your own digging.

- **Media** your business will use to reach the target audience. The media may include Internet marketing, Internet radio, conventional radio, trade shows, public speaking, networking, television, magazines, periodicals, flyers, or any other type of engaging media that has the potential to touch your target audience.

- **Buying patterns** of your target market. The first steps are to identify the needs of the potential consumers, conduct research in order to see how to address their needs, review the possibilities, and identify the person or persons that can put your offering in front of buyers.

- **Trends** that affect your potential customers, coupled with fundamental features of any secondary markets. As with the primary target market, it is important to pinpoint the needs, demographics and developing trends that are going to affect the secondary markets later.

Include information about any of the market tests already completed in this section. Specific details should be included in the Appendix. Market studies usually include the target customers who were contacted, all data or information that was provided to prospective customers, how critical satisfying their needs really is, and the target market's willingness to purchase products or services at a blend of different price-points from your business.

If appropriate, detail lead-time considerations. Lead-time is the required amount of time from when a customer places an order until the moment the product or service is delivered. When you research this information, determine your lead-times regarding initial orders, re-orders, and bulk purchases.

While conducting a competitive analysis (often called a SWOT Analysis— Strengths, Weaknesses, Opportunities and Threats), it is critical to identify the competition's product lines or services and market segment. Use this information to determine their strengths and weaknesses, understand the relationship between your target market and your competitors, and identify any opportunities and threats that may affect how you will enter the marketplace.

Also, be certain that you identify all of the primary competitors for each of the products or services offered. For each key competitor, determine their market share. Then try to predict when new competitors will enter into the marketplace. How long will your window of opportunity last? Finally, pinpoint any additional or less impactful competitors that may have an effect on your success. Your competitors' strengths or competitive advantages might become advantages that you too provide. These strengths can be found in many different areas of the business. They typically include:

- An ability to service customers' needs

- The ability to hold a great deal of market share (consumers' brand awareness comes with that)

- Years in business as a trusted organization

- Great financial position, ensuring that they can survive as a business through thick and thin

- Exceptional management or personnel

Weaknesses are easy to understand, as they are simply the opposite of strengths. However, it is important to analyze the same areas as you did for strengths, in order to determine the weaknesses of your competition. Do they satisfy the needs of their customers? What is their current market penetration? How well do the target audiences and the public view them in regard to past performance, trust, and reputability? Are they experiencing financial constraints or limitations? These could all be red flags for any business. If you discover weak spots in the competition, learn why these problems exist, so you can avoid them.

In the event that your target audience is not shared with your competition, you should be able to grow your idea with little resistance. However, if the competition is hungry for your target market, too, you should plan to handle the known roadblocks on your way to success. Some issues you may uncover include:

- High start-up costs

- Significant time required to get your idea off the ground

- Constantly evolving technologies

- Shortage of skilled personnel

- Customers unfamiliar with your company, product or service

- Current intellectual property laws such as patents and trademarks which may inhibit your ability to innovate

The last section that requires research here is the section covering restrictions and regulations. This includes information related to employees, customers, government regulations, and any other future changes. Important items that need to be addressed include steps necessary to conform to any current or pending requirements that affect your business, as well as the timeframe involved. When does your business have to be in compliance? On what date do these changes take effect? What resources do you need in order to conform?

* * *

The COMPANY DESCRIPTION is Part Three of your business plan. While keeping the finer details limited, provide the reader with a brief understanding of how all of the different components of your business work together. A company description typically provides information about the fundamentals of the business, along with a breakdown of the key factors that will lead to the business's success.

When providing the fundamentals of the business, it is important to include detail on the needs of the marketplace that you are trying to satisfy. Ensure you provide detail on the initiatives that you expect will satisfy these needs. Last, provide a breakdown of key individuals and major organizations that have these needs.

Fundamental factors of success typically include an ability to satisfy your customers' needs better than the competition, time- and cost-effective processes of providing products or services, valuable personnel, and quite often, a prime location. Any, or all, of these can be a competitive advantage.

* * *

The ORGANIZATION AND MANAGEMENT section is Part Four to a well-written business plan. This section provides profiles of key members of management. At a minimum, it should include an organization chart that shows the structure of the organization, profiles of key management and Board of Directors (if you have one), and other important ownership information.

The initial subsection of the Organization and Management portion of the business plan should describe structure of your organization. The most effective and cleanest way to show the company's structure is to provide readers with an organizational chart and narrative description. This will demonstrate to your readers that you leave nothing to chance, that a comprehensive plan is in place, and that the most appropriate employee is in charge of each function of the business. Drawing one up can sometimes reveal problems (like who reports to whom, or that one person in fact has two bosses) that you can address before they fester. Potential investors and employees alike find this very important.

Profiles of key management typically follow the organization's structure, listing each key member from top to bottom on your chart. What are the individual roles and responsibilities for members of management? What are their education and employment backgrounds and why are they being brought into the business as a member of the board or senior manager? These details may appear unnecessary in one- or two-person businesses; however, individuals, especially investors, reading the business plan, expect to know everyone's role and level of experience. Provide a well thought-out, detailed write-up, including the function of each department or facet of the business.

One of the most important components for success in the growth of any company is the ability and track record of its owner and management team. Let your readers know about the key people in your company and their backgrounds. Provide résumés that include the following information:

- Name
- Title (include a brief position description along with primary duties)
- Primary responsibilities and authority
- Education
- Unique experience and skills
- Prior employment
- Special skills
- Past track record
- Industry recognition
- Community involvement
- Number of years with the company
- Compensation basis and levels (if you are setting these for the first time, make sure these are reasonable—not too high or too low)

Ensure you quantify achievements (e.g., "Managed a sales force of ten people," "Managed a department of fifteen people," "Increased revenue by 15 percent in the first six months," "Expanded the retail outlets at the rate of two each year," "Improved the customer service as rated by our customers from a 60 percent to a 90 percent rating").

Also, highlight how the people surrounding you complement your own skills. If you're just starting out, show how each person's unique experience will contribute to the success of your venture.

While not all businesses have a Board of Directors, the major benefit of an unpaid advisory board is that it can provide expertise that your company cannot otherwise afford. A board composed of well-known, successful business owners or managers can go a long way toward enhancing your company's credibility and perception of management expertise.

If you have a Board of Directors, be sure to gather the following information when developing your business plan:

- Names

- Positions on the board

- Extent of involvement with the company

- Background

- Historical and future contribution to the company's success

Conclude this section by providing details regarding the legal structure of the business, followed by the ownership information. Is the business incorporated? What type of incorporation is it? Maybe you have an LLC or partnership. Or are you are set up as a sole proprietorship?

The following ownership information is important and necessary for the Organizational Structure section of a successful business plan:

- Owners' names

- Member interest breakdown (who owns how much)

- Company involvement

- Ownership types (such as common and preferred stock, general partner, limited partner)

- Any other existing equity equivalents such as warrants, options, convertible debt, etc.

- Common stock

* * *

The MARKETING AND SALES STRATEGIES section is Part Five of your business plan. Marketing is the process of creating customers, the lifeblood of your business. In this section, the first thing you want to do is define your marketing strategy. There is no single way to approach a marketing strategy. Your strategy should be part of an ongoing business-evaluation process and be unique to your company. However, there are common steps you can follow to help you think through the direction and tactics you would like to use to drive sales and sustain customer loyalty.

An overall marketing strategy should include, at a minimum, these four strategies:

- A market penetration strategy

- A growth strategy. This strategy for building your business might include an *internal* strategy such as how to increase your human resources, an *acquisition* strategy such as buying another business, a *franchise* strategy for branching out, a *horizontal* strategy where you would provide the same type of products to different users, or a *vertical* strategy where you would continue providing the same products but would offer them at different levels of the distribution chain.

- Channels of distribution strategy. Choices for distribution channels could include original equipment manufacturers (OEM's), an internal sales force, distributors, or retailers, licensees, and sister or daughter companies under a larger umbrella.

- Communication strategy. How are you going to reach your customers? Usually, a combination of the following tactics works the best: promotions, advertising, public relations, personal selling, and printed materials such as brochures, catalogs, flyers, etc.

After you have developed a comprehensive marketing strategy, you can then define your sales strategy. This covers how you plan to actually sell your products or services.

Your overall sales strategy should include two primary elements:

- A **sales force strategy**. If you are going to have a sales force, do you plan to use internal or independent representatives? How many salespeople will you recruit for your sales force? What type of recruitment strategies will you use? How will you train your sales force? What about compensation?

- Your **sales activities.** When you are defining your sales strategy, it is important that you break it down into activities. For instance, you need to identify your prospects. Once you have made a list of your prospects, you need to prioritize the contacts, selecting the leads with the highest potential to buy first. Next, identify the number of sales calls you will make over a certain period of time. From there, you need to determine the average number of sales calls you will need to make to win an order, the average sale per order, and the average sale per customer in a given period of time.

* * *

The SERVICE OR PRODUCT LINE section is Part Six of your business plan. What are you selling? In this section, describe your service or product, emphasizing the benefits to potential and current customers. For example, don't tell your readers which 89 foods you carry in your Gourmet-to-Go shop. Tell them why busy, two-career couples will prefer shopping in a service-oriented store that records clients' food preferences and caters to even the smallest parties on short notice.

Focus on the areas where you have a distinct advantage. Identify the problem in your target market for which your service or product provides a solution. Give the reader hard evidence that customers are, or will be, willing to pay for your solution. List your company's services and products and attach any marketing or promotional materials. Provide details regarding suppliers, availability of products or services, and product or service costs. Also include information addressing new products or services which will soon be added to the company's line.

This section should include:

- **A detailed description of your product or service** (from your customers' perspective). You should include information about the specific benefits of your product or service. You should also talk about your product or service's ability to meet consumer needs, or any advantages your offering has over the competition's.

- **Information related to your product's life cycle.** Include information about where your product or service is in its life cycle (e.g. idea, prototype, etc.), as well as any factors that may influence its cycle in the future.

- Any **copyright, patent and trade secret information** that may be relevant. This should include information related to existing, pending or anticipated copyright and patent filings along with any key characteristics of your products or services for which you cannot obtain a copyright or patent. This is where you should also incorporate key aspects of your products or services that may be classified as trade se-crets (while not disclosing the secrets themselves). Last, but not least, be sure to add any information pertaining to existing legal agreements, such as nondisclosure or non-compete agreements.

- **Research and development (R&D) activities** you are involved in or are planning to be involved in, including any in-process or future activities related to the development of new products or services. This section should also cover information about what you expect the results of future R&D activities to be. Be sure to analyze the R&D efforts of not only your own business, but also that of others in your industry.

* * *

The FUNDING REQUEST is Part Seven of your business plan, if that is your purpose for this version of your plan. In this section, you will request the amount of funding you will need to start or expand your business. If necessary, you can include different funding scenarios, such as best- and worst-case scenarios. Remember that later, in the Financial section (see below), you must be able to back up these requests and scenarios with corresponding financial statements.

You will want to include the following in your funding request:

- Your **current** funding requirement
- Your **future** funding requirements over the next five years
- **How you will use** the funds you receive
- Any **long-range financial strategies** that you are planning that would impact your funding request

When you are outlining your current and future funding requirements, ensure you include the amount you want now and the amount you want in the future, the time period that each request will cover, the type of funding you would like to have (e.g., equity, debt), and the terms that you would like to have applied.

How will you use your funds? This is very important to a creditor.

- Is the funding requested for capital expenditures (spending that creates future benefits, e.g., buying new kitchen equipment for your bakery business so that it can produce twice as many baked goods)?
- Is it for working capital (funding the general operations of your business)?
- Is it for debt retirement (paying off all or part of your business's debts)?
- Or acquisitions (purchasing new assets)?

Whatever it is, be sure to list it in this section.

Last of all, ensure that you include any strategic information related to your business that may impact your financial situation in the future, such as going public with your company, having a leveraged buyout, being acquired by another company. Explain the method by which you will service your debt, or whether or not you plan to sell your business in the future. Each of these is extremely important to a future creditor, since they will directly affect your ability to repay your loan(s) or influence the use of other funding.

* * *

The FINANCIALS section is Part Eight of your business plan. The financials should be developed after you've analyzed the market and set clear, realistic objectives. Only then can you allocate resources efficiently. The following is a list of the critical financial statements to include in your business plan packet:

Historical Financial Data. If you own an established business, you must supply historical data on your company's performance. Most creditors request data for the last three to five years, depending on the length of time you have been in business.

The historical financial data to include are your company's income statements (a list of sales, expenses, and profit for a given period), balance sheets (a summary of a business's financial condition, including assets, liabilities and net worth), and cash flow statements (statements, each for a given period, illustrating cash receipts and cash payments for a business) for each year you have been in business (usually for up to three to five years). Often, creditors are also interested in what collateral (personal assets pledged to secure a business loan) you may have, regardless of the stage of your business.

Prospective Financial Data. All businesses, whether start-up or growing, should supply prospective financial data. Most of the time, creditors will want to see what you expect your company to be able to do over the next five years. Each year's documents should include forecasted income statements, balance sheets, cash flow statements, and capital expenditure budgets (money spent to acquire or upgrade physical assets such as buildings and machinery). For the first year, you should supply monthly or quarterly projections. Thereafter, you can stretch it to quarterly and/or yearly projections for years two through five.

Ensure that your projections match your funding requests. Creditors are always on the lookout for inconsistencies. It's much better if you catch mistakes before they do. If you have made assumptions in your projections, be sure to summarize what you have assumed. This way, your reader will not be left guessing.

Finally, include a short analysis of your financial information. Include a ratio and trend analysis (compare the performance of different periods of time in order to highlight your business's growth) for all of your financial statements (both historical and prospective). Since pictures speak louder than words, you may want to add graphs of your trend analysis, especially if they are positive.

* * *

The APPENDIX, Part Nine, is the final section of your business plan. However, this section should be provided to readers only on an as-needed basis. In other words, it should *not* be included with the main body of your business plan. Your plan is your communication tool. As such, it will be seen by a lot of people. You will not want *everyone* to see some of the information in this section. Specific individuals (such as creditors) may want access to this information in order to make lending decisions. Therefore, it is important to keep it separate—yet to have the Appendix within easy reach.

The Appendix should include:

- Credit history (personal and business)
- Résumés of key managers
- Product pictures and other graphics
- Letters of reference
- Details of market studies
- Relevant magazine articles or book references
- Licenses, permits or patents
- Legal documents
- Copies of leases
- Building permits
- Contracts
- List of business consultants, including attorney and accountant

As we noted above, the distribution of your business plan should be controlled. Do ensure that you keep and maintain an accurate distribution record. This will allow you to update and maintain your business plan as needed. Also, ensure that you include a private placement disclaimer with your business plan if you plan to use it to raise capital (funding to run the operations of your business).

Afterword:
Where to Go from Here?

IT MAY BE SAFE TO ASSUME that if you've just finished reading this book, you are one of two types of individuals. The *curious* reader may have been interested in learning how a potentially successful business could be envisioned, created and then finally launched to compete in the marketplace. For curious readers, these pages may have even sparked your imagination about becoming an entrepreneur one day. Curious readers have always shown interest in educating and informing themselves on a new topic and enhancing their knowledgebase while doing so.

The *serious* reader may have chosen to read our book because he or she may have already decided to toss a hat in the ring and become an entrepreneur. Or perhaps, you've launched your business, and now additional tools, expert guidance, and real-world examples of business finance are vital to your success. A serious reader never stops perusing every possible source for innovative ideas, the next greatest trend, or even a leg up on the competition.

Curious or serious, we hope that everyone who has read this fourth volume of our series found the material worthy of your time. Regardless of how or why you found us, we are glad you did.

For the guys who wrote this volume, and also founded the Expert Business Advice website, the philosophy was simple:

- Create material of substance and value that can continue to be expanded indefinitely for the benefit of the reader, the customer, and the business professional
- Deliver the best possible ideas, resources and guidance to those who seek it
- Take ownership of our work, stand by it, and be proud of it

Developing this material from several points of view and delivering it to people from diverse backgrounds and with multiple levels of experience was crucial for us. In fact, it was the only way we could imagine doing it.

Simply put, our goal with this series shares the same vision as our own company's slogan: "Experts Create | We Deliver | You Apply."

The way forward begins here...

Acknowledgements

WE HAVE A LOT OF THANKS TO GIVE.

Scott wishes to thank his wife Kellin, his co-authors, his parents, the Girard Family, the Conway Family, the Edwards Family, the Seaman Family, the Warren Family (keep up the writing, Lea), the O'Keefe Family, the Thomas Family, the Price Family, everyone at Pinpoint Holdings Group, Barbara Stephens, Jack Chambless, Mary-Jo Tracy, Sandra McMonagle, Diane Orsini, Nathan Holic, Peter Telep, Pat Rushin, and the Seminole Battalion.

Mike wishes to thank his parents Tim and Gaye O'Keefe, his co-authors, Jamie, Kimberly Rupert, the O'Keefe Family, the Goldsberry Family, the Roy Family, the Hubert Family, the Murat Family, the Grant Family, the Girard Family, the Price Family, the Holycross Family, the most inspiring professor Jack Chambless, his two favorite authors Clive Cussler and Timothy Ferriss, and those individuals in Argentina (for making sure there is always Malbec on the table).

Marc wishes to thank his wife Dawn; his co-authors; his mom Lynda; the Price Family; the O'Bryan Family; the Smith Family; Jean Hughes; the O'Keefe Family; the Girard Family; Mike Schiano; David Wittschen and Family; Kurt Ardaman; Axum Coffee in Winter Garden, Florida; and his life-long mentor, Howard Satin.

The authors would collectively like to thank Kathe Grooms and everyone at Nova Vista Publishing, everyone at Expert Business Advice, Jon Collier, and the Van Beekum Family: Dave, Melissa and the Sugar Gliders.

Glossary

Note: We are pleased that this book is being marketed worldwide. However, that means that you may encounter financial terms in your country that differ from some that we commonly use. We suggest that if you need help, you visit the many web sites that provide simple definitions and short, informative articles for extra help.

Accountant	One who is trained and qualified in the practice of accounting or who is in charge of public or private accounts.
Accounting	The systematic recording, reporting and analysis of the financial transactions of a business or government.
Accredited Investor	A term defined by various countries' securities laws that characterizes investors permitted to invest in certain types of higher risk investments including seed money, limited partnerships, hedge funds, private placements, and angel investor networks. The term generally includes wealthy individuals and financially-oriented organizations such as banks, insurance companies, significant charities, some corporations, endowments, and retirement plans.
Acquisitions	Acquiring control of a business, called a target, by stock purchase or exchange, either hostile or friendly. Also called a takeover.
Administrative Expenses	Necessary expenses associated with the general operation of an organization that cannot be attributed to any one department or business unit.
Alpha	A coefficient which measures risk-adjusted performance, factoring in the risk due to the specific security, rather than the overall market. Alpha personalities are dominant in groups, in contrast with Betas.
Amortize	To write or pay off of debt in regular installments over a period of time, often related to an asset's lifetime.
Angel Investor	An individual who provides funding to one or more start-up companies. The individual is usually affluent or has a personal interest in the success of the venture. Such investments are distinguished by high levels of risk and a potentially large return on investment.

Annual Report Audited document required by the Securities Exchange Commission in the U.S. and sent to a public company's or mutual fund's shareholders at the end of each fiscal year, reporting the financial results for the year (including the balance sheet, income statement, cash flow statement and description of company operations) and commenting on the outlook for the future.

Audit An examination and verification of a business's financial and accounting records and supporting documents by a tax professional or governmental tax regulatory authority.

Balance Sheet A quantitative synopsis of a company's financial condition at a specific point in time, including assets, liabilities and net worth. The first part of a balance sheet illustrates all the productive assets a company owns, and the second part shows all the financing methods (such as liabilities and shareholders' equity). Also called a statement of condition.

Ball-Park Figure A figure given as an estimated value based on information available. Also called a ball park estimate.

Benchmark A standard, used for comparison.

Bid Bond A bond purchased by a business or individual when bidding on a large project or sale, in order to demonstrate that sufficient funding exists to complete the transaction if the bidder is selected. The bond guarantees that the bidder will not be prevented from fulfilling the contract by availability by lack of funding.

Bond A debt security, under which the issuer owes the holders a debt and, depending on the terms of the bond, is obliged to pay them interest and/or to repay the principal at a later date.

Bonding Company A financial entity, most commonly an insurance company, which assumes the risk of a surety bond obligee by guaranteeing payment on the bond in the event of a default or a failure of the obligee to perform its contracted services.

Bookkeeping The systematic transcription of a business's financial transactions.

Bottom Line The amount left after taxes, interest, depreciation, and other expenses are subtracted from gross sales. Also called net earnings, net income, or net profit.

Brain-Trust Equity Equity that is accepted or earned through an individual's contribution of information, ideas, or concepts to the strategic growth, development or direction of a company and its products, services or organizational structure.

Bribery	The act or practice of giving or accepting a something of value in exchange for a favor.
Broker	An individual or firm who acts as an intermediary between a buyer and seller, typically charging a commission.
Budget	An itemized prediction of an individual's or business's income and expenses expected for some period in the future.
Budget Deficit	The amount by which a business or individual's spending exceeds its income over a specific period of time.
Business Model	A description of the operations of a business including the segments of the business; its functions, roles and relationships; and the revenues and expenses that the business generates.
Business Operations	Ongoing recurring activities involved in running a business in order to generate value for its stakeholders.
Business Plan	A document prepared by a company's founder or management, or by a consultant on their behalf, that details the past, present, and future of the company, usually for the purpose of attracting capital investment.
Business Taxes	Taxes owed and paid by a corporate entity.
Buyer	In general terms, a person or entity who purchases some good or service from another.
Buyout	The purchase or acquisition of controlling interest in one corporation by another corporation, in order to take over assets and/or operations.
Capital	1. Cash or goods used to produce income either by investing in a business or a different income property.
	2. The net worth of a company; that is, the amount by which its assets exceed its liabilities.
	3. The money, property, and other valuables which collectively represent the value of an individual or business.
Capital Requirements	The amount of cash a business needs for its normal operations.
Carrying Cost	The total cost of holding inventory.
Cash Capital Disbursement	The repaying of a debt or expense.
Cash Flow	The movement of money into or out of a business.
Cash Flow Negative	When costs exceed income.

Cash Flow Positive When income exceeds liabilities.

Cash Flow Statement A summary of a business's cash flow over a given period of time.

Cash Position The amount of cash available to a company at a given point in time.

Class A Office Space These buildings represent the highest quality buildings available. They are generally the most attractive buildings with the best construction, and possess high quality building infrastructure. Class A buildings also are well-located, have good access, and are managed by professionals.

Class B Office Space One notch down from Class A quality, Class B buildings are generally a little older, but are still well-managed. Often, value-added investors target these buildings as investments, since well-located Class B buildings can be returned to their Class A status through renovation such as façade and common area improvements.

Closing a Sale The resolute conclusion and completion of a sale. When one party agrees to pay, or pays, another for goods and/or services.

Collateral Assets pledged by a borrower to secure a loan or other credit, and subject to seizure in the event of default. Also called security.

Commission A fee charged for a service in facilitating a transaction, such as the buying or selling of securities, goods or real estate.

Consumer A person who buys products or services for personal use and not for manufacture or resale.

Contingency Plan A plan devised for an outcome other than the one in the expected plan.

Contract A binding agreement between two or more parties for taking action, or refraining from taking action, sometimes in exchange for lawful monetary or other consideration.

Controlling Interest The ownership of a majority of a company's voting stock; or a significant fraction, even if less than the majority, if the rest of the shares are not actively voted.

Convertible Debt Security which can be converted for a specified amount of another, related security, at the option of the issuer and/or the holder. Also called convertible.

Corp. The abbreviation for *corporation*.

Corporation	The most common form of business organization, which is given many legal rights as an entity separate from its owners. This form of business is characterized by the limited liability of its owners, the issuance of shares of easily transferable stock, and existence as a going concern.
Cost-Effective	Giving adequate and favorable value when compared with the original cost.
Credentials	A tangible representation of qualification, competence, or authority issued to an individual by a third party with a relevant authority or assumed competence to do so.
Credit	The borrowing ability of an individual or company.
Credit History	A record of an individual's or company's past borrowing and repaying behavior.
Credit Line	An amount of credit extended to a borrower.
Credit Report	A report comprised of detailed information on a person's credit history.
Credit Score	A numerically represented measure of credit risk calculated from a credit report using a standardized formula.
Credit Worthiness	A creditor's measure of an individual's or company's ability to meet debt responsibilities.
Crowd Funding	Funding a business by raising many small amounts of money from a large number of people.
Debt	An amount owed to a person or organization for funds borrowed.
Debt Financing	Financing by selling bonds, bills or notes to individuals or businesses.
Debt Retirement	The repayment of a debt.
Debt-to-Income Ratio	A figure that calculates how much income is spent repaying debts.
Deduction	An expense subtracted from adjusted gross income when calculating taxable income. Also called tax deduction.
Depreciate	Diminish in value over a period of time.
Direct Cost	Cost of materials, labor related to the production of a product.
Discount	To sell anything below its normal price.

Distributor	An entity which buys from a producer and then sells and delivers merchandise to retail stores, or acts as an intermediary in business. Sometimes called a *wholesaler* or *middleman*.
Diversification	A portfolio strategy designed to reduce risk by combining a variety of investments, such as stocks, bonds, and real estate, which are unlikely to all move in the same direction.
Dividend	A taxable cash award declared by a company's board of directors and given to its shareholders out of the company's current or retained earnings, usually quarterly. Also used as a slang term to mean reward.
Double Taxation	Taxation of the same income at two levels. One common example is taxation of earnings at the personal income level and then again at the sales level.
Downsizing	Diminishing the total number of employees at a company through terminations, retirements, or spinoffs.
Economics	The study of how the forces of supply and demand assign scarce resources.
Economy	Activities related to the production and distribution of goods and services in a specific geographic region.
EFS	Acronym for Electronic Filing System.
Employee	A person hired to provide services to a company on a regular basis in exchange for compensation and who does not provide these services as part of an independently owned business.
Entrepreneur	An individual who starts his or her own business.
Equity	Ownership interest in a business in the form of common stock or preferred stock.
Equity Financing	Financing a business by selling common or preferred stock to investors.
Expansion	Growth.
Expenditure	A payment, or the guarantee of a future payment.
Expense	Any cost of conducting business.
Expense Report	A document that contains all the expenses that a business has incurred as a result of the business's operation.
Fair Isaac Corporation	A publicly traded company that provides analytics and decision making services, including credit scoring, intended to help financial services companies make complex, high-volume decisions.

Fair Price	A price for a product or service that is comparable to fair market value.
Fee	A charge for products delivered or services rendered.
FICO	Acronym for Fair Isaac Corporation.
Financial Adviser	A person or organization employed by a business or mutual fund to manage assets or provide investment advice.
Financials	Documents related to finance.
Financing	Providing the necessary monetary capital.
Fixed Expense	An expense that does not change depending on production or sales levels, such as rent, property tax, insurance, or interest expense. Also called fixed cost.
Forecast	A prediction based on historic data and current knowledge used to estimate the direction of future trends.
Forfeiture	The act of forfeiting.
Free Market	Business governed solely by the laws of supply and demand, not restrained by government interference, regulation or subsidy.
Funding Request	A request for funding.
GAAP	See Generally Accepted Accounting Principles.
General Partner	A partner with unlimited legal obligation for the debts and liabilities of a partnership.
Generally Accepted Accounting Principles (GAAP)	A set of standards, conventions, and rules that accountants follow in recording and summarizing and in the preparation of financial statements.
Global Marketplace	All business-related transactions that take place between two or more regions, countries and nations beyond their political boundary.
Globalization	Processes of international integration arising from increasing human connectivity and interchange of worldviews, products, ideas, and other aspects of business culture.
Grant	Funds disbursed by the grantor to a recipient.
Gross Margin	A measure of profitability, often shortened to GM. To calculate divide Gross Income by Net Sales, and express it as a percentage. For example, a widget sells for $5 and costs $3 to make.

$5 (Net Sales) - $3 (Cost of Goods) = $2 (Gross Income).

Then $2 \div 5 = 0.4$, which expressed as a percentage is 40% Gross Margin.

Growth Rate	A measure of financial growth.
Growth Strategy	A plan of action based on investing in companies and sectors which are growing faster than their peers. Also can mean an organization's plan for increasing, expanding, and otherwise getting bigger.
High-Net-Worth Individual	A person who owns considerable assets; usually used in connection with donations, loans and investments.
IFRS	See International Financial Reporting Standards.
Inc.	Abbreviation for incorporated.
Income	Revenues minus cost of sales, operating expenses, and taxes, over a given period of time.
Incorporated	A business that has been formed into a legal corporation by completing the required procedures.
Indemnity Bond	An insurance bond used as an additional measure of security to cover loan amounts, worth about 75 percent of the value of the property. This bond protects lenders from loss, in the event that the borrower defaults on the loan.
Indirect	Not directly caused by or resulting from something, as in indirect costs.
Initial Public Offering	The initial sale of stock by a company to the public.
Interest	The return earned on an investment.
Internal Revenue Service	The federal agency of the United States responsible for administering and enforcing the U.S. Treasury Department's revenue laws, through the assessment and collection of taxes, determination of pension plan qualification, and related activities.
International Financial Reporting Statement (IFRS)	A common global accounting practice that is used in many countries worldwide.
International Securities Identifier Number	A exclusive international code which identifies a securities issue.
Investment Banker	An individual who acts as an underwriter or agent for businesses and municipalities issuing securities.
Investment Group	A group of investors who pool some of their money and make joint investments. Also called an investment club.

Investor	An individual who commits monetary capital to investment products with the expectation of financial return.
IPO	Acronym for Initial Public Offering.
IRS	Acronym for Internal Revenue Service.
ISIN	Acronym for International Securities Identifier Number.
Joint Venture	A contractual agreement joining together two or more entities for the purpose of executing a particular business undertaking.
Key Financial Driver	Unique to every company, any influencer that could materially affect a company's finances.
Late Payment Fee	Commonly called a "late charge", a fee charged to a borrower who misses paying at least their minimum payment by the payment's deadline.
Legal Representation	An attorney. Also called a lawyer.
Lender	A person or organization who lends money.
Lending Portfolio	A collection of investments all owned by the same person or organization.
Leveraged Buyout	The takeover of a company or controlling interest of a company (a buyout), involving a significant amount of borrowed (leveraged) money.
Liability	An obligation that legally commits an individual or company to settle a debt.
Licensing	Under defined conditions, the granting of permission to use intellectual property rights, such as trademarks, patents, or technology.
Limited Liability Company	A type of company, authorized only in certain business sectors, whose owners and managers receive the limited liability and tax benefits of an S-Corporation without having to conform to S-Corporation restrictions.
Limited Partner	In a corporate entity with one or more general partners, limited partners are liable only to the extent of their investments. Limited partners also enjoy rights to the partnership's cash flow, but are not liable for company obligations.
Liquidation	The process of converting assets or investments into cash.
Liquidity	The ability of an asset or property to be converted into cash quickly and without any price discount.
LLC	Acronym for limited liability company.

Loan   An arrangement in which a lender gives monetary capital or property to a borrower, and the borrower agrees to return the property or repay the monetary capital, usually along with interest, at some future point in time.

Manpower   The set of individuals who make up the workforce of an organization.

Manufactured Cost   The total cost of producing a product, including the direct labor costs, direct material costs, overhead costs, and any other expenses associated with production.

Market Analysis   Research intended to predict the expectations of a market.

Marketing Plan   A written document that illustrates the necessary actions to achieve one or more marketing objectives. It can be for a product or service, a brand, or a product line.

Market Share   The percentage of the total sales of a given type of product or service that is won by given company.

Market Test   A geographic region or demographic group used to gauge the applicability of a product or service in a marketplace, prior to a wide-scale launch.

Mentor   A more experienced or more knowledgeable person who helps to guide a less experienced or less knowledgeable person.

Merchant Banking   An investment bank which is well-equipped to manage multinational corporations. Commonly, electronic.

Middleman   Intermediary between two commercial entities, commonly a wholesaler or distributor who buys from a manufacturer and sells to a retailer or to consumer.

NDA   Acronym for non-disclosure agreement.

Negative Cash Flow   When costs exceed liabilities.

Net Profit   Actual profit after working expenses not included in the calculation of gross profit have been paid.

Non-Disclosure Agreement A contract that prohibits the disclosure of confidential information or proprietary knowledge under specific circumstances.

Non-Profit Company   An organization created to accomplish specified goals but without the intention of making profits, unlike a commercial organization. Its shareholders or trustees do not benefit financially. Some non-profits plow any potential profits back into their future budgets to avoid becoming profitable.

Offering	A general term for the output of a business; the goods or services it sells.
Operating Expense	An expense arising in the normal course of running a business, such as manufacturing, advertising and sales.
OPEX	Acronym for operating expense.
Opportunity Cost	The cost of passing up the next best choice when making a decision.
Outsourcing	Work executed for a business by people other than the business's full-time employees.
Ownership Equity	The owner's share of the assets of a business.
Partners	Members of a partnership, either general or limited.
Partnership	A relationship of two or more entities, people or companies, conducting business for mutual benefit.
Payment Bond	A surety bond through which a contractor assures an owner that material and labor provided in the completion of a project will be fully paid for, and that no mechanics' liens will be filed against the owner.
Payment Terms	The conditions under which a seller allows a buyer to pay off the amount due in a transaction.
Performance Bond	A bond issued to guarantee adequate and acceptable completion of a project by a contractor.
Personal Finances	One's private funds, property, possessions. The application of finance principles to the monetary decisions of a person or family.
Placement	The selling of new securities. Can also refer to temporary employment with a company.
Positive Cash Flow	When income is greater than costs.
Price Point	A point on a range of possible prices at which something might be marketed.
Principle	A rule or ethical standard.
Private Labeling	A retailer's name, as used on a product sold by the retailer but manufactured by another company.
Private Placement	The sale of shares directly to an institutional investor, such as a bank, mutual fund, insurance company, pension fund, or foundation.

Private Placement Disclaimer   A disclaimer that specifies that the sale of securities directly to an institutional investor, such as a bank, mutual fund, foundation, insurance company, etc. does not require Securities Exchange Commission (SEC) registration, provided that the securities are purchased for investment purchases only, not for resale.

Product   The end result of the manufacturing process.

Productivity   The calculated amount of output per unit of input.

Profit   The positive gain from an investment or business operation after deducting all expenses.

Pro Forma   Description of financial statements that have one or more assumptions or hypothetical conditions built into the data. Often used with balance sheets and income statements when data is not available, to construct scenarios. One variety is called a Pro Forma Income Statement. Another is a Pro Forma Invoice.

Projections   Quantitative estimates of prospective economic or financial performance.

Promissory Note   A document signed by a borrower promising to repay a loan under agreed-upon terms. Also called a note.

Publicly Traded Company   A company with a fixed number of shares outstanding.

Ratio   The result of one value divided by another.

Ratio Analysis   The study and interpretation of the relationships between various financial variables, used often by investors or lenders.

Return on Investment (R.O.I.)   Benefit yielded by an investment when compared to its cost, usually expressed as a ratio or percentage.

Revenue   The total amount of money received by an organization for goods or services provided during a certain time period. Sometimes called turnover.

Risk   The quantifiable probability of loss or less-than-expected returns.

Risk/Reward   A calculated measurement of the degree of risk inherent in a given investment in relation to the potential profit associated with it.

R.O.I.   See Return on Investment.

S-Corporation   A type of corporation, recognized in the US by the Internal Revenue Service for most companies with 75 or fewer shareholders, which enables the company to enjoy the benefits of incorporation but be taxed as if it were a partnership. Also called Subchapter S Corporation, or S-Corp.

Sales	Total monetary amount collected for goods and services provided.
SBA	Acronym for the Small Business Administration in the US.
SBA Loan	A business loan issued by the US Small Business Administration.
S.E.C.	See United States Securities and Exchange Commission.
Selling Expenses	Costs associated with the sales process.
Service	A type of economic activity that is intangible, is not stored, and does not result in any kind of ownership. Examples are health care, training or entertainment.
Shareholder	One who owns shares of stock in a corporation or mutual fund. For corporations, along with the ownership comes a right to declared dividends and the right to vote on certain company matters, including the board of directors. Also called a stockholder.
Small Business Administration	A US Federal agency which offers loans to small businesses.
Socioeconomics	Referring to social and economic conditions, social classes and income groups.
Sole Proprietorship	A company which is not registered with the state as a limited liability company or corporation and is a business structure in which an individual and his/her company are considered a single entity for tax and liability purposes.
Sponsorship	Financial or other support, often for a specific event, program, or project, that may give the sponsor an opportunity to advertise.
Stakeholder	Anyone who is interested in or affected by something; one who could benefit from information about it. Not to be confused with shareholders.
Start-Up	1. The beginning of a new company or new product. 2. A new, usually small business that is just beginning its operations, especially a new business supported by venture capital and in a sector where new technologies are used.
Start-Up Capital	The initial stage in financing a new project, which is followed by several rounds of investment capital as the project gets under way
Statement of Cash Flows	A summary of a company's cash flow over a given period of time. Also called Cash Flow Statement.
Strategy	A planned system of action targeting a goal or outcome.
Subsidy	Financial aid given by the government to individuals or groups.

Supply Chain	All the elements that combine to transform raw input into something an end-consumer can buy, including materials, knowledge, people, technology, transporters, distributors, retailers, etc. Can apply to intangible as well as tangible items.
Surety Bond	A bond issued by an entity on behalf of a second party, guaranteeing that the second party will fulfill an obligation or series of obligations to a third party. In the event that the obligations are not met, the third party can recover its losses via the bond.
Sustainability	The capacity to endure.
SWOT Analysis	An assessment of an organization's strengths, weaknesses, opportunities and threats.
Takeover	Acquiring control of a corporation, called a target, by stock purchase or exchange, either hostile or friendly.
Target Market	The selection of a market that will be the most advantageous segment in which to offer a product or service. Also called a market target.
Tax Implications	Conditions or actions that can affect the amount of taxes payable.
Taxes	A fee levied (charged) by a government on a product, income, or activity.
Terms	Related to sales, loans and payments, the conditions or obligations two parties agree to for a purchase; may include timing of payments, delivery, etc.
Time Management	The act or process of planning and exercising conscious control over the amount of time spent on specific activities, especially to increase effectiveness, efficiency or productivity.
Top Line	Refers to the first line of an income statement, generally reserved for gross sales or revenue. "Top-line" growth is synonymous with "revenue growth".
Trade Show	A marketing, fair-like event at which goods and services in a specific industry are exhibited, demonstrated and sold.
Trading Platform	Software provided by a stock broker in order to buy and sell shares in the stock market.
Transparency	Conditions under which facts are fully and accurately disclosed in a timely manner.
True Cost	The bottom-line figure when information is collected and presented for each proposed alternative. Can also mean the fully loaded cost of an item.

Under-Capitalized	An entity that lacks sufficient operating capital to perform well.
Underwriting	The procedure by which an underwriter brings a new security issue to the investing public in an offering. In such a case, the underwriter will guarantee a certain price for a certain number of securities to the party that is issuing the security. Thus, the issuer is secure that they will raise a certain minimum from the issue, while the underwriter bears the risk of the issue.
United States Securities and Exchange Commission	An independent federal agency that oversees the exchange of securities in the United States to protect investors.
Variable Expense	A cost of labor, material or overhead that changes according to the change in the volume of production units. Combined with fixed costs, variable costs make up the total cost of production. Also called variable cost.
Venture Capitalist	An investor who engages in venture capital projects. Venture capitalists seek opportunities involving businesses that are growing or are in risky market segments, since these businesses generally have a harder time obtaining loans. Frequently called VCs.
Web-Based Business	A company that does most of its business on the Internet, usually through a website that uses the popular top-level domain, *.com*. Also called an Internet business, web business, dot-com company, or simply a dot-com.
Wholesale	The purchase of goods in quantity for resale purposes. Also called wholesale distribution.
Wholesale Distribution	See *wholesale*.
Working Capital	Current liabilities subtracted from current assets. Working capital measures the liquid assets a company has available to build its business.
Yield	The annual rate of return on an investment, expressed as a percentage.

Resources

ExpertBusinessAdvice.com

At **ExpertBusinessAdvice.com**, our goal is to become your complete resource for simple, easy-to-use business information and resources. Enjoy reading about techniques and processes necessary to develop and grow your business. **ExpertBusinessAdvice. com** offers an array of tools and resources to help you along the way by offering tutorials, downloadable templates, real-life examples, and customer support. You can even email us and a qualified member of our staff (yes, a real person!) will review your inquiry and get back to you. Now you can take charge of your professional growth and development, learn from others' success, and make a dramatic positive impact on your business. Learn the principles and practices that seasoned professionals use, at **ExpertBusinessAdvice.com,** for free!

THE WAY FORWARD BEGINS HERE...

Want to learn how to start a business? Are you looking for an additional income stream? No problem—we can get you started down the right path. Do you want to know how to plan, creating the necessary documents to obtain financing for your business? Maybe you just want to learn how experienced business leaders streamline financial models, maximize output, inspire managers, and incentivize employees, tapping the full range of resources available. Regardless of your needs, **ExpertBusinessAdvice. com** is here for you!

www.expertbusinessadvice.com

CRASH COURSE for ENTREPRENEURS

Many novice entrepreneurs have little more than a brilliant idea and a pocketful of ambition. They want to know *Now what?* This 12-title series tells *exactly what you must know*, in simple terms, using real-world examples. Each two-hour read walks you through a key aspect of being an entrepreneur and gives practical, seasoned, reader-friendly advice.

Whether your dream business is dog walking or high-tech invention, home-based or web-based, these books will save you time and trouble as you set up and run your new company. Collectively, these three young Florida-based serial entrepreneurs have successfully started seventeen new companies across a broad range of sectors and frameworks, including finance, international sourcing, medical products, innovative dot-com initiatives, and traditional brick-and-mortar companies.

A Crash Course for Entrepreneurs—From Expert Business Advice

Starting a Business – Everything you need to build a new business, starting from scratch.
Sales and Marketing – Solid guidance on successfully developing and promoting your business and its brand.
Managing Your Business – Proven techniques in managing employees and guiding your business in the right direction.
Business Finance Basics – Tax tips, funding resources, money management, basic accounting, and more!
Business Law Basics – A must-know overview on types of businesses, risks and liabilities, required documents, regulatory requirements, and the role of a business attorney. *Co-Author: Mark R. Moon, Esq.*
Franchising – A how-to guide for buying and running a franchise business.
Value-Driven Business – Value is the muscle behind every successful business. Here's how to introduce it into your operation.
Time and Efficiency – Wheel-spinning is the most destructive force in business. Make the most of your time to maximize income and motivate employees.
International Business – The world is a big place filled with billions of potential partners and customers. This guide offers tips to reach them all.
Supplemental Income – Can't commit full time? No problem! Here's how to make extra money in your spare time.
Social Media – This rapidly-growing networking and advertising medium is changing the world. Here's how to use it to grow your business.
Web-Based Business – The biggest, most valuable companies out there today are Internet businesses. Here's why, and how you can build one yourself.
Paperback and eBook format available. 160 pages, 6 ½" × 9" (16.5 × 23 cm), US$18.95, with extensive glossary and index.

www.expertbusinessadvice.com **www.novavistapub.com**

Index

Tip: We suggest you check the Glossary (pages 165-79) for definitions related to items in this index.

About the Authors

Scott L. Girard, Jr.

Editor-in-Chief, Expert Business Advice, LLC
Email: scott@expertbusinessadvice.com

Before joining Expert Business Advice, Scott was Executive Vice President of Pinpoint Holdings Group, Inc., where he directed multiple marketing and advertising initiatives. Scott was a key player for the Group, negotiating and facilitating the sourcing logistics for the commercial lighting industry division, which supplied clients such as Gaylord Palms, Ritz Carlton, Marriott, Mohegan Sun, and Isle of Capri with large-scale lighting solutions. His vision and work were also pivotal in the growth and development of Bracemasters International, LLC.

Scott has degrees in Business Administration and English Writing and is a published contributor to various periodicals on the topics of economics and politics. He is also a co-author and series editor of *A Crash Course for Entrepreneurs* book series. A graduate of the United States Army Officer Candidate School, Scott is a combat veteran, having served a tour in Kuwait and Iraq as an infantry platoon leader in support of Operation Iraqi Freedom and Operation New Dawn.

Originally from Glendale, California, Scott now lives in St. Petersburg, Florida with his wife and son. Scott is a regular contributor to www.expertbusinessadvice. com. His side projects include a collection of fiction short stories and scripts for two feature films. His motto: "Words have meaning."

Michael F. O'Keefe

Chief Executive Officer, Expert Business Advice, LLC
Email: mike@expertbusinessadvice.com

In 2004, Michael founded O'Keefe Motor Sports, Inc. (OMS Superstore), eventually growing it into one of the largest databases of aftermarket automotive components available on the web. Currently, aside from his position at Expert Business

Advice, LLC, Michael is the President of Pinpoint Holdings Group, Inc. and the Vice President of Marketing for Bracemasters International, LLC.

At Pinpoint Holdings Group, Inc., Michael focuses on strategically building a diverse portfolio of assets including technology, biomedical and traditional brick-and-mortar companies, as well as commercial and residential real estate. He also played a key role in facilitating the logistics of the commercial lighting branch of the company, bridging the gap between Pinpoint's office in Wuxi, China, and their commercial clients.

Recently, Michael's passion and talents for contemporary business techniques and practices were demonstrated in the exponential growth of Bracemasters International, LLC. Michael developed dynamic marketing campaigns, web-based marketing strategies, and e-Commerce initiatives resulting in Bracemasters' website viewership growing by 17,000 percent in just under two years and its annual revenues growing by over 100 percent. Michael's talent, leadership ability, and prospective vision make him a vital player in the contemporary business arena.

Michael holds degrees in both international business and real estate with a focus on commercial real estate development and finance. He credits over 20 years of competitive sailing with his father as the reason for his tactical and highly strategic approach to business structure, growth strategy, and leadership.

Originally from Delavan, Wisconsin, Michael now resides in Orlando, Florida.

Marc A. Price

Director of Operations, Expert Business Advice, LLC
Email: marc@expertbusinessadvice.com

Marc has collaborated with the Federal Government, United States Military, major non-profit organizations, and some of the largest corporations in America, developing and implementing new products, services and educational programs. Equally skilled in Business-to-Business and Business-to-Consumer functions, Marc has facilitated product positioning, branding and outreach efforts on many different platforms for the organizations he has worked with.

As an entrepreneur, Marc has successfully directed the launch of seven different companies, ranging from traditional brick-and-mortar establishments to innovative dot-com initiatives. Four were entertainment production companies (sound, lighting, staging, logistics, talent, entertainment), one was a business services company serving small companies, one was concerned with business and land acquisition, and two were website and business consulting services. Using his expertise in organizational management and small business development, Marc's latest focus is on working with new entrepreneurs and small-to-medium-sized businesses in emerging industries.

As an accomplished public speaker and writer, Marc has appeared on nationally syndicated television and radio networks, in national print publications, and has been the subject of numerous interviews and special-interest stories. Marc is a regular contributor to www.expertbusinessadvice.com.

Marc received his Bachelor of Science in Organizational Management from Ashford University. He and his wife divide time between Orlando, Florida and elsewhere, including an active schedule of international travel. His motto: "You can't build a reputation on what you are going to do."—Henry Ford

Business Efficiency Resources

Get More Done Seminars

Grooms Consulting Group, a sister company to Nova Vista Publishing, offers proven training that saves professionals one month or more of time wasted on email, information and meeting inefficiency.

• 83% of all professionals are overloaded by email – we can save up to 3 weeks a year, per person
• 92% want to improve their information storage system – we can make searches 25% faster and more successful
• 43% of all meeting time is wasted – we can save up to another 3 weeks per year, per person

> *"We saved 15 days a year!"*
> Matt Koch, Director of Productivity
> Capital One Financial Services

Three Two-Hour Modules: We offer three powerful seminars: **Get Control of Email**, **Get Control of Info**, and **Get Control of Meetings**.
They can be delivered in any combination you wish and can be customized.
Who Should Attend? Anyone who handles email, stores information, and attends meetings. Leaders leverage their position for added impact.
Delivery Options: Seminar, keynote speech, webinar, e-learning, and executive coaching.
Return on Investment (ROI): We can measure the impact of every session on participants with five-minute online pre- and post-surveys. We deliver a report that shows time saved, productivity gained, participant satisfaction, and other significant impacts.

Special pricing is available for groups.

Three *Get More Done* Modules: Combine and Customize as You Wish

1. GET CONTROL OF EMAIL
• Pump up your productivity by eliminating unnecessary email
• De-clutter your jammed inbox
• Write more effective messages
• Discover time-saving Outlook® / Lotus® tech tips
• Improve email etiquette and reduce legal liability
• Choose the best communication tool

2. GET CONTROL OF INFORMATION
• Get organized, once and for all
• Never lose a document again
• File and find your information in a flash; make shared drives productive
• Make better decisions with the right information
• Create an ordered, stress-free folder structure throughout your system

3. GET CONTROL OF MEETINGS
• Meet less and do more through virtual and other advanced options
• Reduce costs, boost productivity and go green with improved, efficient virtual meetings
• Run engaging, productive live meetings
• Discover time-saving e-calendar tips
• Keep every meeting productive and on track, make follow-ups easy

Satisfaction Guaranteed
We guarantee that the vast majority of your people will rate our seminars "excellent" or "good", or your money back.

> *"A huge hit with our people!"*
> Joel Burkholder
> Regional Program Coordinator – ACLCP

Contact: Kathe Grooms
kgrooms@groomsgroup.com

CAREERS
I Just Love My Job!
Roy Calvert, Brian Durkin, Eugenio Grandi and Kevin Martin, in the Quarto Consulting Library (ISBN 978-90-77256-02-2, softcover, 192 pages, $19.95)

Taking Charge of Your Career
Leigh Bailey (ISBN 978-90-77256-13-8, softcover, 96 pages, $14.95)

LEADERSHIP AND INNOVATION
Grown-Up Leadership
Leigh Bailey and Maureen Bailey (ISBN 978-90-77256-09-1, softcover, 144 pages, $18.95)

Grown-Up Leadership Workbook
Leigh Bailey (ISBN 978-90-77256-15-2, softcover, 96 pages, $14.95)

Leading Innovation
Brian McDermott and Gerry Sexton (ISBN 978-90-77256-05-3, softcover, 160 pages, $18.95)

SALES
Win-Win Selling
Wilson Learning Library (ISBN 978-90-77256-34-3, softcover, 160 pages, $18.95)

Versatile Selling
Wilson Learning Library (ISBN 978-90-77256-03-2, softcover, 160 pages, $18.95)

Time Out for Salespeople
Nova Vista Publishing's Best Practices Editors, (ISBN 978-90-77256-14-5 hardcover with marker ribbon, 272 pages, $19.95; ISBN 978-90-77256-31-2 softcover, 272 pages, $14.95)

Get-Real Selling, Revised Edition
Michael Boland and Keith Hawk (ISBN 978-90-77256-32-9, softcover, 144 pages, $18.95)

SCIENCE PARKS, ECONOMICS, ECOLOGY OF INNOVATION
What Makes Silicon Valley Tick?
Tapan Munroe, Ph.D., with Mark Westwind, MPA (ISBN 978-90-77256-28-2, softcover, 192 pages, $19.95)

**Visit www.novavistapub.com for sample chapters, reviews, links and ordering.
eBooks are now available too!**